University of London
Institute of Latin American Studies Monographs

2

Accounts of
Nineteenth-Century South America

University of London
Institute of Latin American Studies Monographs

1. *The 'Detached Recollections' of General D. F. O'Leary*, edited by R. A. Humphreys. 1969
2. *Accounts of Nineteenth-Century South America: an Annotated Checklist of Works by British and United States Observers*, by Bernard Naylor. 1969

Accounts of Nineteenth-Century South America

An Annotated Checklist of Works
by British and United States Observers

by

BERNARD NAYLOR

Librarian,
Institute of Latin American Studies

UNIVERSITY OF LONDON
Published for the
Institute of Latin American Studies
THE ATHLONE PRESS
1969

Published by
THE ATHLONE PRESS
UNIVERSITY OF LONDON
at 2 Gower Street, London WCI
Distributed by Tiptree Book Services Ltd
Tiptree, Essex

Australia and New Zealand
Melbourne University

Canada
Oxford University Press
Toronto

U.S.A.
Oxford University Press Inc
New York

© *University of London,* 1969

485 17702 1

Printed in Great Britain by
WESTERN PRINTING SERVICES LIMITED
BRISTOL

CONTENTS

NOTE

The following references are cited in abbreviated form in the text:

HARVARD UNIVERSITY. Bureau for Economic Research in Latin America: *The economic literature of Latin America: a tentative bibliography.* 2 vols. Cambridge, Harvard University Press, 1935.

JONES, Tom Bard: *South America rediscovered.* Minneapolis, University of Minnesota Press, 1949.

New voyages and travels: consisting of originals, translations and abridgements. Edited by Sir R. Phillips. 9 vols. London, R. Phillips, 1820–1823.

NEW YORK PUBLIC LIBRARY: *Catalogue of the History of the Americas collection.* 28 vols. Boston, G. K. Hall, 1961.

SABIN, Joseph: *A dictionary of books relating to America, from its discovery to the present time.* 29 vols. New York, J. Sabin, 1868–1936.

INTRODUCTION

Travellers' accounts of Latin America in the nineteenth century have long and rightly been considered a historical source of primary importance. In this bibliography I have concerned myself only with the countries of South America from Colombia and Venezuela to Argentina and Chile (but excluding British, French and Dutch Guiana), and only with works written in English.[1] Even so, some further limitation has been necessary. I have sought to include all important descriptions of the South American scene which are based on first-hand experience, and I therefore cite the accounts of British subjects and American citizens who lived in one or another of the South American countries for extensive periods, as well as travel books more narrowly defined. But I have not thought it would be useful to include every narrative, however brief, of every traveller, however transitory. Fifty pages is the customary arbitrary limit used to define a pamphlet, and I have therefore, by that criterion, excluded all pamphlets, all books in which the descriptive content is less than 50 pages, and all periodical articles.

I have divided the century into three more or less arbitrary periods and the continent into four regions. Titles have been put into the period to which they relate, rather than the one in which they were published. And, as far as possible, accounts published outside the century, but relating to it, have been added to the relevant section. Titles which relate to more than one region have been grouped together in a general section.

The details given about each work are: author, title, place of publication, name of publisher, date of publication and pagination. In each case the edition described is the first, except where a later edition is clearly to be preferred on the grounds of relevance to the bibliography. Subsequent editions to the first are

[1] See also, for Mexico, C. H. Gardiner, 'Foreign Travelers' Accounts of Mexico, 1810–1910' (*The Americas* VIII, Jan. 1952, pp. 321–51), for South America, T. B. Jones, *South America Rediscovered* (University of Minnesota Press, 1949), and, for Latin America as a whole, R. A. Humphreys, *Latin American history: a guide to the literature in English* (London, O.U.P., 1958).

described in full whenever the new edition represents a significant alteration or enlargement of the original; otherwise only their existence is mentioned. Titles are transcribed as they appear in the original editions, but, where titles were printed in upper case only, present-day usage has been followed.

The annotations are not intended to supply critical comment about the quality of a book's contents. They do aim to supply any necessary information, not provided by the title, about the subject interest of the book in terms of this bibliography. They also seek to give such information, derived from the books themselves or from other sources, as will help in an assessment of the standing of the author, the kind of information likely to interest him, the degree of authority with which he wrote, and the kind of audience his published work was likely to command. To add further elements to the picture of South America obtained in the United States of America and the United Kingdom, a small section has been added to the bibliography, containing some of the major translations from first-hand observers, writing originally in French, German or Spanish, which became available to the English-speaking public in the nineteenth century. An author index completes the work.

The bibliography is based on a thesis originally submitted to the University College London, School of Librarianship in part requirement for the University of London Diploma in Librarianship. I should like to thank all those librarians and others who, knowingly or unknowingly, helped me in its compilation, and especially Professor R. A. Humphreys, who first suggested the subject to me and was a constant source of encouragement and helpful suggestions.

June 1968   B.N.

I. 1800–1830

(a) General

1. ANDREWS, Joseph

Journey from Buenos Ayres, through the provinces of Cordova, Tucuman, and Salta, to Potosi, thence by the deserts of Caranja to Arica, and, subsequently, to Santiago de Chili and Coquimbo, undertaken on behalf of the Chilian and Peruvian Mining Association in the years 1825–26. 2 vols. London, John Murray, 1827. xxxii, 312; viii, 321 p.

2. BENNETT, Thomas H.

A voyage from the United States to South America, performed during the years 1821, 1822 & 1823. Embracing a description of the city of Rio Janeiro, in Brazil; of every port of importance in Chili; of several in Lower Peru; and of an eighteen months cruise in a Nantucket whaleship. The whole Interspersed with a variety of Original Anecdotes. Newburyport, Herald Press, 1823. 86 p.

The edition described is the second, said to contain 'some alterations and additions' to the first. Some subsequent editions appeared under the title: *Chile and Peru in 1824.* The edition described was published anonymously. The New York Public Library attributes this to Washington Chase.

3. BRACKENRIDGE, Henry Marie

Voyage to South America, performed by order of the American government, in the years 1817 and 1818, in the frigate Congress. 2 vols. Baltimore, John Toy for the author, 1819. 351; 381 p. map.

A lawyer and author, Brackenridge was brought into the U.S. diplomatic service specifically to study the South American political situation. He acted as secretary to the commissioners who visited South America on behalf of the United States government, 1817–19. The *Dictionary of American Biography* describes him as 'an intelligent and liberal participant in public affairs and an enlightened commentator on them'. In the English edition of 1820 (London, John Miller) the chapters are arranged differently. *Cf.* items 28, 41 and 59.

4. CALDCLEUGH, Alexander

Travels in South America, during the years 1819–20–21; containing an account of the present state of Brazil, Buenos Ayres, and Chile. 2 vols. London, John Murray, 1825. xii, 373; viii, 380 p. maps, illus.

Caldcleugh was a promoter of the Anglo-Chilean Mining Company.

5. CLEVELAND, Richard Jeffry

A Narrative of voyages and commercial enterprises. 2 vols. Cambridge, Mass., John Owen, 1842. xvi, 249; viii, 240 p.

Cleveland is described by the *Dictionary of American Biography* as 'one of the greatest of the great race of New England sea captains'. His numerous voyages took place between 1797 and 1821. He later served as U.S. vice-consul in Havana (1828–33). This book contains material on Rio de Janeiro, Valparaiso, Lima and the Río de la Plata.

6. COCHRANE, Thomas (10th Earl of Dundonald)

Narrative of services in the liberation of Chile, Peru and Brazil from Spanish and Portuguese domination. 2 vols. London, James Ridgway, 1859. xxii, 293; xi, 305 p.

Cochrane had a noteworthy career as a naval officer in the Revolutionary and Napoleonic wars and as a persistent critic of naval abuses of the time. But after being accused of connivance in a Stock Exchange fraud he was expelled from the Navy, Parliament and the Order of the Bath. He commanded the Chilean navy from 1819 to 1822 and was an admiral in the Brazilian navy from 1823 to 1825. Subsequently reinstated in the Royal Navy, he continued his vigorous and controversial career, attaining the rank of Admiral in 1851. *Cf.* item 62.

7. DAVIE, John Constanse

Letters from Buenos Ayres and Chile with an original history of the latter country. By the author of Letters from Paraguay. London, R. Ackermann, 1819. xi, 323 p. illus.

Published anonymously. Jones (*South America Rediscovered*) thinks the narrative is probably fictional, though he considers the local colour accurate, on the whole. *Cf.* item 29.

8. HAIGH, Samuel

Sketches of Buenos Ayres and Chile. London, J. Carpenter, 1829. xviii, 316 p.

A merchant adventurer, Haigh was a friend of Woodbine Parish and General William Miller. He fought with the Chilean forces at the battle of Maipú. A second edition (London, Effingham Wilson, 1831, x, xiv, 434 p.) was entitled *Sketches of Buenos Ayres, Chile and Peru*. Substantially the same text as the first, it contains, in addition, a new title-page and contents list and a supplementary section on Peru.

9. HEAD, Francis Bond

Rough notes taken during some rapid journeys across the Pampas and among the Andes. London, John Murray, 1826. xii, 309 p.

Head served in the Royal Engineers from 1811 to 1825 and was present at the battle of Waterloo. From 1825 to 1826 he was manager of the Río de la Plata Mining Association. Later he became Lieutenant-Governor of Upper Canada, and was created a baronet in 1836 and a Privy Councillor in 1867. *Cf.* item 33.

10. HIBBERT, Edward

Narrative of a journey from Santiago de Chile to Buenos Aires in July and August 1821. London, John Murray, 1824. 146 p. map.

Hibbert travelled north of the usual route across the pampas. The work was published anonymously.

11. MATHISON, Gilbert Farquhar

Narrative of a visit to Brazil, Chile, Peru and the Sandwich Islands during the years 1821 and 1822. With miscellaneous remarks on the past and present state and political prospects of those countries. London, Charles Knight, 1825. xii, 478 p. map, illus.

12. MAW, Henry Lister (Lieutenant R.N.)

Journal of a passage from the Pacific to the Atlantic, crossing the Andes in the northern provinces of Peru, and descending the River Marañon, or Amazon. London, John Murray, 1829. xv, 486 p. map.

13. MIERS, John

Travels in Chile and La Plata, including accounts respecting the geography, geology, statistics, government, finances, agriculture, manners and customs, and the mining operations in Chile. Collected during a residence of several years in these countries. 2 vols. London, Baldwin, Cradock and Joy, 1826. xv, 494; vii, 532 p. maps, illus.

Engineer, botanist and Fellow of the Royal Society, Miers accompanied Lord Cochrane to Chile in 1818. He tried unsuccessfully to develop Chilean mineral deposits.

14. MOULTON, William

A concise extract, from the sea journal of William Moulton; written on board of the Onico, in a voyage from the port of New-London in Connecticut, to Staten-Land in the South Sea; together with strictures and remarks on various subject matters which came within his notice, on the coast of South America, and at a variety of islands in the South Sea and Pacific Ocean, in the years, 1799, 1800, 1801, 1802, 1803, and 1804. Printed at Utica for the Author, 1804. 158 p.

This entry is derived from Sabin (51136) and the Library of Congress catalogue.

15. PORTER, David (Captain, U.S.N.)

Journal of a cruise made to the Pacific Ocean by Captain David Porter in the United States frigate 'Essex' in the years 1812, 1813, 1814. Containing Descriptions of the Cape de Verd Islands, Coasts of Brazil, Patagonia, Chili and Peru, and of the Gallapagos Islands; also, a full Account of the Washington Groupe of Islands, the Manners, Customs, and Dress of the

Inhabitants etc. etc. 2 vols. Philadelphia, Bradford and Ins-
keep, 1815. viii, 263; 169 p. maps, plans, illus.

Porter was the first U.S. naval officer to show American
colours in the Pacific, where he campaigned against British
whalers. After outstanding successes, his ship the *Essex* sur-
rendered to a superior British force following a fierce and desper-
ate struggle outside the harbour of Valparaiso. His subsequent
career included a spell as first Commissioner of the U.S. Navy
Board and as Commander-in-Chief of the West Indies Squad-
ron. Following a quarrel with the naval authorities he resigned
his commission but retained the respect of the government
sufficiently to be appointed to diplomatic posts in the Middle
East.

16. PROCTOR, Robert
Narrative of a journey across the cordillera of the Andes, and
of a residence in Lima and other parts of Peru, in the years 1823
and 1824. London, Hurst and Robinson, Edinburgh, Archibald
Constable, 1825. xx, 374 p.
Proctor was agent for a British loan to Peru.

17. SALVIN, Hugh
Journal written on board of His Majesty's Ship Cambridge
from January, 1824, to May, 1827, by the Rev. H. S., Chaplain.
Newcastle, Edward Walker, 1829. 245 p. front.
H.M.S. *Cambridge* took out the first British consuls to South
America.

18. SHILLIBEER, John
A narrative of the Briton's voyage to Pitcairn's Island.
Taunton, J. W. Marriott for the author, London, Law and
Whittaker, 1817. iii, 179 p. illus.
Contains material on Rio de Janeiro, Chile and Peru.

19. SPANISH AMERICA and the United States; or, Views of
the actual commerce of the United States with the Spanish
colonies, and of the effects of a war with Spain on that commerce. Also some observations on the probable influence of the
emancipation of the Spanish colonies on the agriculture and

commerce of the United States. By a merchant of Philadelphia. Philadelphia, M. Carey, 1818. 58 p.

'We have made a long and tedious tour round the coast of Spanish America, from Vera Cruz to Acapulco . . .'—Page 56.

20. SPANISH AMERICA. Observations of an American upon the works of M. de Pradt on the actual state of America. London. Printed by R. Wilks and sold by E. Wilson, Rodwell, and J. Booth, 1817. 76 p.

'Having lately passed through this part of the globe, I shall give an account of what I have seen.'

21. STEWART, Charles Samuel

A visit to the South Seas, in the U.S. ship Vincennes, during the years 1829 and 1830; with scenes in Brazil, Peru, Manilla, the Cape of Good Hope, and St. Helena. 2 vols. New York, John P. Haven, 1831. xi, 357; iv, 360 p.

Stewart was chaplain. *Cf.* item 117.

22. THOMSON, James

Letters on the moral and religious state of South America, written during a residence of nearly seven years in Buenos Aires, Chile, Peru, and Colombia. London, James Nisbet, 1827. vi, 296 p.

23. WALTON, William

Present state of the Spanish colonies: including a particular report of Hispañola, or the Spanish part of Santo Domingo: with a general survey of the settlements on the South continent of America, as relates to history, trade, population, customs, manners, etc. with a concise statement of the sentiments of the people on their relative situation to the mother country etc. by William Walton Jun., Secretary to the expedition which captured the city of Santo Domingo from the French; and resident British agent there. 2 vols. London, Longman, Hurst, Rees, Orme and Brown, 1810. xiv, 384; vii, 386 p. map, illus.

Walton claims his account of mainland South America is based on first-hand knowledge.

24. WEBSTER, William Henry Bayley

Narrative of a voyage to the Southern Atlantic Ocean in the years 1828, 29, 30, performed in H.M. Sloop Chanticleer, under the command of the late Captain Henry Foster, F.R.S. etc. by order of the Lords Commissioners of the Admiralty. 2 vols. London, Richard Bentley, 1834. xi, 399; viii, 398 p. maps, illus.

Webster was a surgeon. His account gives extensive descriptions of the east coast of South America, and includes Venezuela and Colombia.

(b) Río de la Plata Region

25. An AUTHENTIC NARRATIVE of the proceedings of the expedition under the command of Brigadier-Gen. Craufurd, until its arrival at Monte Video; with an account of the operations against Buenos Ayres under the command of Lieut.-Gen. Whitelocke. By an officer of the expedition. London, published by the author, 1808. viii, 216 p. maps, plans.

This is sometimes attributed to Captain Joseph Thomson.

26. An AUTHENTIC NARRATIVE of the proceedings of the expedition against Buenos Ayres, under the command of Lieut. Gen. Whitelocke. By an Irish Officer. Dublin, R. Smith and W. Figgis, 1808. 109 p.

27. BEAUMONT, J. A. B.

Travels in Buenos Ayres and the adjacent provinces of the Rio de la Plata with observations intended for the use of persons who contemplate emigrating to that country; or, embarking capital in its affairs. London, James Ridgway, 1828. xii, 270 p. map.

28. BRACKENRIDGE, Henry Marie

Voyage to Buenos Aires performed in the years 1817 and 1818, by order of the American government. London, Sir Richard Phillips, 1820. iv, 130 p.

This is to be found in volume 3 of *New Voyages and Travels* and consists of extracts from Brackenridge's two-volume work, item 3. *Cf.* also items 41 and 59.

29. DAVIE, John Constanse

Letters from Paraguay: describing the settlements of Montevideo and Buenos Ayres; the presidencies of Rioja Minor, Nombre de Dios, St. Mary and St. John etc., etc. with the manners, customs, religious ceremonies etc. of the inhabitants. Written during a Residence of seventeen Months in that Country. London, G. Robinson, 1805. vii, 293 p.

Cf. item 7.

30. FERNYHOUGH, Thomas

Military memoirs of four brothers (natives of Staffordshire) engaged in the service of their country as well in the new world and Africa, as on the continent of Europe, by the survivor. London, William Sams, 1829. xi, 275 p.

This item contains material on the British actions in the Río de la Plata area, 1806–7. The third edition (London, Joseph Masters, 1838, xi, 324 p.), though more extensive, contains no added material of significance to this topic.

31. FRACKER, George

A voyage to South America with an account of a shipwreck in the river La Plata in the year 1817 by the Sole Surviver. Boston, Ingraham and Hewes, 1826. vi, 7–128 p.

Published anonymously. In his preface to the edition examined, the author makes reference to 'the former edition', of which I have found no trace.

32. GILLESPIE, Alexander

Gleanings and remarks: collected during many months of residence at Buenos-Ayres, and within the upper country; with a prefatory account of the expedition from England, until the Surrender of the Colony of the Cape of Good Hope, under the joint command of Sir D. Baird, G.C.B., K.C., and Sir Home Popham, K.C.B. Leeds, B. Dewhirst for the author, 1818. ii, 342 p. map, chart.

Contains material on the British occupation of Buenos Aires 1806–7. Gillespie was a major in the Royal Marines.

33. HEAD, Francis Bond

Reports relating to the failure of the Rio Plata Mining Association, formed under an authority signed by his excellency Don Bernardino Rivadavia. London, John Murray, 1827. vii, 228 p. map.

Cf. item 9.

34. KING, John Anthony

Twenty-four years in the Argentine republic; embracing the author's personal adventures, with the civil and military history of the country, and an account of its political condition, before and during the administration of Governor Rosas; his course of policy; the causes and character of his interference with the government of Monte Video, and the circumstances which led to the interposition of England and France. London, Longman, Brown, Green and Longmans, 1846. xii, 442 p.

'An officer in the army of the republic'—Title-page. Appleton of Philadelphia published an American edition in the same year.

35. LOVE, George Thomas

A five years' residence in Buenos Ayres, during the years 1820 to 1825: containing remarks on the country and inhabitants; and a visit to Colonia del Sacramento. By an Englishman. With an appendix, containing rules and police of the port of Buenos Ayres, Navigation of the River Plate etc. etc. London, G. Hebert, 1825. viii, 176 p.

Love was editor of the *British Packet* in Buenos Aires. This book was published anonymously. There was a second edition in 1827.

36. MACDOUALL, John (R.N.)

Narrative of a voyage to Patagonia and Terra del Fuego, through the Straits of Magellan, in H.M.S. 'Adventure' and 'Beagle', in 1826 and 1827. London, Renshaw and Rush, 1833. iv, 320 p. front.

37. A NARRATIVE OF FACTS connected with the change effected in the political condition and relations of Paraguay,

under the directions of Dr. Thomas [*sic*] Francia, by an individual who witnessed many of them, and obtained authentic information respecting the rest. London, W. Mason, 1826. 56 p.

38. A NARRATIVE OF THE OPERATIONS of a small British force under the command of Brigadier General Sir Samuel Auchmuty, employed in the reduction of Montevideo on the River Plate A.D. 1807 by a field officer on the staff. London, John Joseph Stockdale, 1807. 60 p. map.

The British Museum attributes this to J. G. P. Tucker.

39. NOTES ON THE VICEROYALTY of La Plata, in South America; with a sketch of the manners and character of the inhabitants, collected during a residence in the city of Monte Video, by a gentleman recently returned from it. To which is added, a history of the operations of the British troops in that country, and biographical and military anecdotes of the principal officers employed in the different expeditions. London, J. J. Stockdale, 1808. 301 p. maps, front.

40. POPHAM, Home Riggs (Sir)

A full and correct report of the trial of Sir Home Popham, including the whole of the discussions which took place between that officer and Mr. Jervis, the Counsel for the Admiralty, who acted upon this occasion as prosecutor, and also the observations of the several members of the court. Together with a preface, containing a further Vindication of Sir Home Popham, particularly against certain Attacks made upon him since the Trial: and an appendix, in which are Several important Documents, which have never been published; and among others an interesting Letter from Lord Grenville to Sir Home Popham. London, J. and J. Richardson, 1807. xxxii, 224 p.

A naval officer, Popham shared with General Sir David Baird the command of an expedition which successfully captured the Cape of Good Hope in 1806. He then joined with Colonel (later Viscount, General) William Carr Beresford in an unauthorised attack on Buenos Aires in which, after initial successes, Beresford and his force were captured by the Spaniards. Though court-martialled and reprimanded, Popham continued his naval career, being awarded the K.C.B. in 1815 and retiring in 1820 with the rank of Rear Admiral. The book also contains an unpaginated appendix.

41. RODNEY, Caesar Augustus *and* GRAHAM, John

The reports on the present state of the United Provinces of South America; drawn up by Messrs Rodney and Graham, commissioners sent to Buenos Ayres by the government of North America, And laid before the Congress of the United States; with their accompanying documents; occasional notes by the editor; and an introductory discourse, intended to present, with the reports and documents, a view of the present state of the country, and of the progress of the independents. London, Baldwin, Cradock and Joy, 1819. viii, 358 p. map.

Rodney had wide experience in the public service. He was a member of the U.S. Congress and Senate and served in the army in the war of 1812. He was also President Jefferson's Attorney General. Later he became first U.S. minister plenipotentiary in Buenos Aires.

Graham, too, was a public servant who enjoyed the confidence of President Jefferson. Named minister plenipotentiary to Portugal (but to reside in Brazil) he spent less than a year in Rio de Janeiro where the climate had an adverse effect on his health.

The third commissioner was Theodorick Bland. *Cf.* items 3, 28 and 59.

42. VIDAL, Emeric Essex

Picturesque illustrations of Buenos Ayres and Monte Video, consisting of twenty-four views: accompanied with descriptions of the scenery, and of the costumes, manners etc. of the inhabitants of those cities and their environs. London, R. Ackermann, 1820. xxviii, 115 p. illus.

At the time, Vidal was purser of H.M.S. *Hyacinth*.

43. WEDDELL, James (Master R.N.)

A voyage towards the South Pole, performed in the years 1822–24, containing an examination of the Antarctic sea to the seventy-fourth degree of latitude: and a visit to Tierra del Fuego, with a particular account of the inhabitants. To which is added much useful information on the coasting navigation of Cape Horn, and the adjacent lands, with charts of harbours etc. London, Longman, Hurst, Rees, Orme, Brown and Green, 1825. iv, 276 p. maps, illus.

Weddell was a distinguished seaman and navigator who quickly surmounted the early setback of imprisonment for mutiny. Admiral of the Fleet Sir George Rose Sartorius described him as 'one of the most efficient and trustworthy officers I have met with in the course of my professional life'. The second edition (London, 1827) contains in addition: *Observations on the probability of reaching the South Pole, and an account of a second voyage performed by the Beaufoy, Captain Brisbane, to the same seas.*

44. WHITELOCKE, John

The proceedings of a general court martial, held at Chelsea hospital, on Thursday, January 28, 1808, And continued, by Adjournment, till Tuesday, March 15, for the trial of Lieut. Gen. Whitelocke, Late Commander-in-Chief of the Forces in South America. Taken in short-hand by Mr. Gurney. With the defence, copied from the original, by permission of General Whitelocke; also all the documents produced on the trial. 2 vols. London, Longman, Hurst, Rees and Orme, 1808. 8, 438, xxxix; 8, 439–830 p. maps.

Whitelocke commanded the force which tried unsuccessfully to redeem the situation caused by the defeat of Beresford (item 40). Defeated and forced to withdraw from Buenos Aires, he was court-martialled and cashiered.

45. YATES, William

A brief relation of facts and circumstances connected with the family of the Carrera in Chile: with some account of the last expedition of Brigadier General Jose Miguel Carrera, his death etc. London, 1824.

This constitutes an appendix to Maria Graham's *Journal of a Residence in Chile* (item 65). Yates was an Irish adventurer who fought in the civil war in Argentina 1820–21.

(c) Brazil

46. ARMITAGE, John

The History of Brazil, from the period of the arrival of the Braganza family in 1808, to the abdication of Don Pedro the First in 1831. Compiled from state documents and other original sources. Forming a continuation to Southey's History of that country. 2 vols. London, Smith and Elder, 1836. xv, 371; viii, 297 p. fronts.

Armitage's account derives partly from a first-hand acquaintanceship with Brazil.

47. ASHE, Thomas

A commercial view and geographical sketch of the Brasils in South America and of the island of Madeira. London, Allen, 1812. 160 p.

'Who travelled the continent of America several years'—Note on the title-page.

48. CHAMBERLAIN, Henry

Views and costumes of the city and neighbourhood of Rio de Janeiro, Brazil, From Drawings taken by Lieutenant Chamberlain, Royal Artillery, During the Years 1819 and 1820, with descriptive explanations. London, Thomas McLean, 1822.

The book consists of 36 lithographs with accompanying text.

49. GRAHAM, Maria (Lady Callcott)

Journal of a voyage to Brasil and residence there during parts of the years 1821, 1822, 1823. London, Longman, Hurst, Rees, Orme, Brown and Green and John Murray, 1824. vi, 335 p. illus.

Née Dundas, Maria Graham was married successively to Thomas Graham, who died in 1822, and, in 1827, to Sir Augustus Wall Callcott. She became the tutor of Dona Maria, daughter of the Emperor Pedro I of Brazil. Maria later succeeded to the throne of Portugal when her father renounced his own claims. *Cf.* item 65.

50. HENDERSON, James

A History of the Brazil; comprising its geography, commerce, colonization, aboriginal inhabitants etc. etc. etc. London, Longman, Hurst, Rees, Orme and Brown, 1821. xxiii, 522 p. maps, illus.

'Recently from South America'—Note on the title-page. Henderson also served for a time as consul-general in Colombia.

51. KOSTER, Henry

Travels in Brazil. In the years from 1809 to 1815. London, Longman, Hurst, Rees, Orme and Brown, 1816. ix, 501 p.

Koster had a familiarity with Portuguese due to his childhood in Lisbon, and ostensibly travelled to Brazil for health reasons, though at times it is clear that he has an interest in commercial matters. His account mainly concerns Pernambuco. He later became a friend of Robert Southey, to whom the book is dedicated.

A further edition was published in 2 volumes in 1817 in London (Longman etc.) and Philadelphia (H. Carey). It was paginated xii, 406; iv, 380.

52. LINDLEY, Thomas

Narrative of a voyage to Brazil; terminating in the seizure of a British vessel, and the imprisonment of the author and the ship's crew, by the Portuguese. With general sketches of the country, its natural productions, colonial inhabitants, etc and a Description of the City and Provinces of St. Salvador and Porto Seguro. To which are added, A Correct Table of the Latitude and Longitude of the Ports on the Coast of Brazil, Table of Exchange, etc. London, J. Johnson, 1805. xxxi, 298 p.

53. LUCCOCK, John

Notes on Rio de Janeiro and the southern parts of Brazil; taken during a residence of ten years in that country, from 1808 to 1818. London, Samuel Leigh, 1820. xv, 639 p. maps.

A merchant in Lisbon, where he represented Luptons of Leeds, Luccock was forced to transfer his business activities to Rio de Janeiro in 1808. He was primarily a wool dealer, but in Brazil showed a readiness to trade in any commodity which seemed likely to offer a profit. The year 1818 saw his final return to England.

54. MAWE, John

Travels in the interior of Brazil, particularly in the gold and diamond districts of that country, by authority of the Prince Regent of Portugal; including a voyage to the Rio de la Plata, and an historical sketch of the revolution of Buenos Ayres. London, Longman, Hurst, Rees, Orme and Brown, 1812. vii, 368 p. map, illus.

A mineralogist and sailor, Mawe visited Brazil in 1809 and 1810. He was also imprisoned for a time in Montevideo in 1805–6. There was a second edition in 1825 paginated x, 493.

55. SIDNEY, Henry

The travels and extraordinary adventures of Henry Sidney, in Brazil, and the interior regions of South America, in the years 1809, 1810, 1811, and 1812. London, Sold by J. Ferguson, 1815. iv, 159 p.

56. TUCKEY, James Kingston

An account of a voyage to establish a colony at Port Philip in Bass's Strait, on the South Coast of New South Wales, in His Majesty's Ship Calcutta in the years 1802–3–4. London, Longman, Hurst, Rees and Orme, Portsmouth, Mottley, 1805. xv, 239 p.

Tuckey was First Lieutenant of the *Calcutta* and later attained the rank of Commander. An account of Brazil occupies pages 40 to 113.

57 WALSH, Robert

Notices of Brazil in 1828 and 1829. 2 vols. London, Frederick Westley and A. H. Davis, 1830. xv, 528; xii, 541 p. maps, illus.

Walsh was chaplain to the British Embassy in Rio de Janeiro.

(d) West Coast

58. BEECHEY, Frederick William

Narrative of a voyage to the Pacific and Beering's Strait, to co-operate with the Polar Expeditions: performed in His Majesty's Ship Blossom under the command of Captain F. W. Beechey, R.N., in the years 1825, 26, 27, 28. London, Henry Colburn and Richard Bentley, 1831. xxi, 742 p.

A description of Concepción is the main item of interest. Beechey later attained the rank of Rear-Admiral.

59. BLAND, Theodorick

The present state of Chili, from the report laid before Congress by Judge Bland, The Commissioner sent to that Country by the Government of the United States, in 1818. London, J. M. Richardson, 1820. iv, 83 p.

This edition was specially prepared for the English public and omits some of the material in the American edition. *Cf.* items 3, 28 and 41.

60. BOWERS, William (Lieutenant R.N.)

Naval adventures during thirty-five years' service. 2 vols. London, Richard Bentley, 1833. xv, 302; xi, 302 p.

Contains material on Chile and Peru as well as information about such leaders of the independence movement as O'Higgins and San Martín.

61. BRAND, Charles (Lieutenant R.N.)

Journal of a voyage to Peru: a passage across the Cordillera of the Andes, in the winter of 1827, performed on foot in the snow; and a journey across the pampas. London, Henry Colburn, 1828. xvii, 346 p. illus.

Also contains some material on Chile and Argentina.

62. COCHRANE, Thomas (10th Earl of Dundonald)

Memoranda of naval services in the liberation of Chili and Peru from Spanish domination. London, James Ridgway, 1858. xiii, 293 p.

A separate edition of the first volume of item 6.

63. COFFIN, Isaac Foster

Journal of a residence in Chili. By a Young American,

detained in that country, during the revolutionary scenes of 1817–18–19. Boston, Wells and Lilly, 1823. 237 p.

Published anonymously.

64. DELANO, Amasa

A narrative of voyages and travels in the Northern and Southern Hemispheres: comprising three voyages round the world; together with a voyage of survey and discovery, in the Pacific Ocean and Oriental Islands. Boston, R. G. House for the author, 1817. 600 p.

The *Dictionary of American Biography* describes Delano as an 'author and ship's captain' and spells his Christian name Amassa. The book contains material on Chile and Peru.

65. GRAHAM, Maria (Lady Callcott)

Journal of a residence in Chile during the year 1822. And a voyage from Chile to Brazil in 1823. London, Longman, Hurst, Rees, Orme, Brown and Green and John Murray, 1824. v, 512 p. illus.

Cf. items 45 and 49.

66. HALL, Basil (Captain R.N.)

Extracts from a journal written on the coasts of Chile, Peru and Mexico in the years 1820, 1821, 1822. 2 vols. Edinburgh, Archibald Constable, London, Hurst, Robinson, 1824. xviii, 372; xi, 288, 65 p. map.

A man of wide interests, Hall accompanied Lord Amherst's Chinese embassy. Among other interesting events in his career were his interview with Napoleon and his observations on the pendulum. He was made a Fellow of the Royal Society in 1816. The work went into several editions.

67. JOHNSTON, Samuel Burr

Letters written during a residence of three years in Chili, containing an account of the most remarkable events in the revolutionary struggles of that province. With an interesting account of the loss of a Chilian ship, and brig of war, by mutiny, and the consequent imprisonment and sufferings of several citizens of the

United States, for six months in the dungeons of Callao. Erie (Pennsylvania), R. I. Curtis, 1816. 205 p. illus.

Entry taken from the *History of the Americas* catalogue of the New York Public Library.

68. MILLER, John

The Memoirs of General Miller, in the service of the republic of Peru. 2 vols. London, Longman, Rees, Orme, Brown and Green, 1828. xxiii, 389; vii, 460 p. maps, illus.

'Compiled chiefly from the private letters, journals, and recollections of my brother, General Miller . . .'—Introduction.

General William Miller began his military career in the field train department of the Royal Artillery, and served in the Peninsula 1811–14. He distinguished himself in the struggle for Chilean independence, and by a cavalry charge at the battle of Ayacucho. Reaching the rank of general of division and commander-in-chief of cavalry, he later served as governor of Potosí (1825) and was finally made a grand marshal of Peru. In 1843, he became British consul-general to the Sandwich Islands. John Miller, too, travelled widely in South America. The same publishers issued a second and fuller edition in 1829.

69. SCHMIDTMEYER, Peter

Travels into Chile, over the Andes, in the years 1820 and 1821, with some sketches of the productions and agriculture; mines and metallurgy; inhabitants, history, and other features, of America; particularly of Chile and Arauco. London, Longman, Hurst, Rees, Orme, Brown and Green, 1824. 379 p. illus., maps.

70. STEVENSON, William Bennet

A historical and descriptive narrative of twenty years' residence in South America, in three volumes; containing travels in Arauco, Chile, Peru and Colombia; with an account of the revolution, its rise, progress and results. London, Hurst, Robinson, Edinburgh, Constable and Oliver and Boyd, 1825. xii, 439; viii, 434; vii, 467 p. illus.

'Formerly private secretary to the president and captain general of Quito, colonel, and governor of Esmaraldas, Captain de Fragata, and late secretary to the Vice admiral of Chile, His Excellency the Right Honourable Lord Cochrane, etc.'—Title-page.

71. SUTCLIFFE, Thomas

Sixteen years in Chile and Peru, from 1822 to 1839. By the retired governor of Juan Fernandez. London, Paris, Fisher, 1841. xii, 563 p. map, illus.

Published anonymously. Sutcliffe held military and administrative positions in Chile.

72. TEMPLE, Edmond

Travels in various parts of Peru, including a year's residence in Potosi. 2 vols. London, Henry Colburn and Richard Bentley, 1830. xvi, 431; viii, 504 p. maps, illus.

Temple was employed by the Potosí, La Paz and Peruvian Mining Association which collapsed in 1826.

(e) North

73. ADAM, William Jackson

Journal of voyages to Marguaritta, Trinidad, and Maturin, with the author's travels across the plains of the Llaneros, to Angustura, and subsequent descent of the Orinoco in the years 1819 and 1820; comprising his several interviews with Bolivar, the supreme chief: sketches of the various native and European generals: and a variety of characteristic Anecdotes, hitherto unpublished. Dublin, R. M. Tims, 1824. 160 p.

74. BACHE, Richard

Notes on Colombia, taken in the years 1822–3, with an itinerary of the route from Caracas to Bogota; and an appendix. By an officer of the United States Army. Philadelphia, Carey and Lea, 1827. 303 p. map.

75. BIGGS, James

The history of Don Francisco de Miranda's attempt to effect a revolution in South America, by a gentleman who was an officer under that general to which are annexed, sketches of the life of Miranda, and geographical notices of Caraccas. Boston, Oliver and Munroe, 1808. xi, 300 p.

Biggs was a member of Miranda's Venezuelan expedition of 1806. This edition was published anonymously. A further edition appeared in London, published by the author in 1809 (xvi, 312 p.). It is described on the title-page as 'revised, corrected and enlarged'.

76. BROWN, C.

Narrative of the expedition to South-America, which sailed from England at the close of 1817, for the service of the Spanish patriots: including the military and naval transactions, and ultimate fate of that expedition: also the arrival of Colonels Blosset and English, with British troops for that service, their reception and subsequent proceedings, with other interesting occurrences. London, John Booth, 1819. 194 p.

Brown served as captain of a Venezuelan brigade of light artillery.

77. CAMPAIGNS AND CRUISES, in Venezeula and New Grenada, and in the Pacific Ocean; from 1817 to 1830: with the narrative of a march from the River Orinoco to San Buenaventura on the coast of Choco; and sketches of the west coast of South America from the Gulf of California to the Archipelago of Chilöe. Also, tales of Venezuela: illustrative of revolutionary men, manners and incidents. 3 vols. London, Longman, 1831.

Sometimes attributed to William D. Mahoney or Richard Longeville Vowell.

78. CHESTERTON, George Laval

A narrative of proceedings in Venezuela, in South America, in the years 1819 and 1820; with general observations on the country and people; the character of the Republican government, and its leading members, etc. also a description of the country of Caraccas; of the force of General Morillo; the state of the royalists; and the spirit of the people under their jurisdiction. London, John and Arthur Arch, 1820. x, 257 p.

Chesterton was captain and judge-advocate of the British Legion raised for the service of the republic of Venezuela.

79. COCHRANE, Charles Stuart

Journal of a residence and travels in Colombia, during the years 1823 and 1824. 2 vols. London, Henry Colburn, 1825. xv, 524; viii, 515 p. map, illus.

80. DUANE, William

A visit to Colombia, in the years 1822 and 1823, by Laguayra and Caracas, over the Cordillera to Bogota, and thence by the Magdalena to Cartagena. Philadelphia, Thomas H. Palmer for the author, 1826. 632 p. front.

A journalist, a politician and a friend of President Jefferson, Duane made this journey as a pleasure trip during his retirement.

81. FLINTER, George Dawson

The history of the revolution of Caracas; comprising an Impartial Narrative of the Atrocities Committed by the contending Parties, illustrating the real state of the contest, both in a commercial and political point of view: together with a description of the Llaneros or People of the Plains of South America. London, W. Glindon for the author, 1819. xii, 212 p.

The *Dictionary of National Biography* describes Flinter as a 'soldier of fortune'.

82. HACKETT, James

Narrative of the expedition which sailed from England in 1817, to join the South American patriots; comprising every particular connected with its formation, history, and fate: with observations and authentic information elucidating the real character of the contest, mode of warfare, state of the armies etc. London, John Murray, 1818. xv, 144 p.

Hackett was a lieutenant in a Venezuelan Artillery Brigade.

83. HALL, Francis (Colonel)

Colombia: its present state, in respect of climate, soil, productions, population, government, commerce, revenue, manufactures, arts, literature, manners, education, and inducements to emigration: with an original map: and itineraries partly from

Spanish surveys, partly from actual observation. London, Baldwin, Cradock and Joy, 1824. vi, 154 p. map.

Hall was a hydrographer in the service of the Colombian government.

84. HAMILTON, John Potter (Colonel)

Travels through the interior provinces of Colombia. 2 vols. London, John Murray, 1827. 332; 256 p. map, illus.

Hamilton was one of the commissioners sent from the United Kingdom to Colombia in 1824.

85. HANKSHAW, J.

Letters written from Colombia, during a journey from Caracas to Bogota and thence to Santa Martha, in 1823. London, G. Cowie, 1824. xvi, 208 p. map.

The economic literature of Latin America attributes this to F. Hall, the British Museum to J. Hankshaw. It was published anonymously.

86. HIPPISLEY, Gustavus

A narrative of the expedition to the rivers Orinoco and Apure in South America, which sailed from England in November 1817 and joined the patriotic forces in Venezuela and Caraccas. London, John Murray, 1819. xix, 653 p.

87. MACERONI, Francis

Memoirs of the life and adventures of Colonel Maceroni, late aide-de-camp to Joachim Murat, King of Naples—Knight of the Legion of Honour, and of St. George of the two Sicilies—ex-general of brigade in the service of the republic of Colombia etc. etc. etc. 2 vols. London, John Macrone, 1838. 497; 509, xxi p. front.

88. THE PRESENT STATE of Colombia; containing an account of the principal events of its revolutionary war; the expeditions fitted out in England to assist in its emancipation; its constitution; financial and commercial laws; revenue expenditure and public debt; agriculture; mines; mining and other associations; with a map, exhibiting its mountains, rivers, departments and

provinces. By an Officer, late in the Colombian Service. London, John Murray, 1827. iv, 336 p.

89. RAFTER, M.

Memoirs of Gregor M'Gregor; comprising a sketch of the revolution in New Granada and Venezuela with biographical notices of Generals Miranda, Bolivar, Morillo and Horé, and a Narrative of the Expeditions to Amelia Island, Porto Bello, and Rio de la Hache, interspersed with revolutionary anecdotes. By M. Rafter, late Colonel in the service of New Granada. London, J. J. Stockdale, 1820. xvi, 17–426 p. map, illus.

90. RECOLLECTIONS OF A SERVICE of three years during the war-of-extermination in the republics of Venezuela and Colombia, by an officer of the Colombian navy. 2 vols. London, Hunt and Clarke, 1828. xv, 251; viii, 277 p.

91. ROBINSON, James H.

Journal of an expedition 1400 miles up the Orinoco and 300 up the Arauca; with an account of the country, the manners of the people, military operations, etc. London, Black, Young and Young, 1822. xix, 397 p. illus.

'Late surgeon in the Patriotic Army'—Title-page.

92. SEMPLE, Robert

Sketch of the present state of Caracas; including a journey from Caracas through La Victoria and Valencia to Puerto Cabello. London, Robert Baldwin, 1812. viii, 176 p.

Semple was an enthusiastic traveller who later became a governor under the Hudson's Bay Company.

93. SHERMAN, John H.

A general account of Miranda's expedition, including the trial and execution of ten of his officers. And an account of the imprisonment and sufferings of the remainder of his officers and men who were taken prisoners. New York, McFarlane and Long, 1808. 120 p.

Published anonymously. Sherman was commissioned under Miranda.

94. SMITH, Moses

History of the adventures and sufferings of Moses Smith, during five years of his life; from the beginning of the year 1806, when he was betrayed into the Miranda expedition, until June 1811, when he was nonsuited in an action at law, which lasted three years and a half. To which is added, a biographical sketch of Gen. Miranda. Albany, Packard and Van Benthuysen for the author, 1814. iv, 13–146, [6] p. illus.

95. WATERTON, Charles

Wanderings in South America, the Northwest of the United States and the Antilles in the years 1812, 1816, 1820 and 1824. London, J. Mawman, 1825. vii, 326 p. illus.

Waterton was a naturalist who travelled widely. He visited Spain in 1802 and resided in British Guiana from 1804 to 1812. His later travels embraced the Guianas, Rome, the United States and the West Indies. This book contains material on Venezuela.

II. 1830–1870

(a) General

96. BOLLAERT, William

Antiquarian, ethnological and other researches in New Granada, Equador, Peru and Chile, with observations on the pre-incarial, incarial, and other monuments of Peruvian nations. London, Trübner, 1860. 279 p. illus.

97. COLTON, Walter (U.S.N.)

Deck and port; or incidents of a cruise in the United States frigate Congress to California. With sketches of Rio Janeiro, Valparaiso, Lima, Honolulu, and San Francisco. New York, A. S. Barnes, Cincinnati, H. W. Derby, 1850. 408 p. map, illus.

Colton was the ship's chaplain.

98. CUNNINGHAM, Robert Oliver

Notes on the natural history of the strait of Magellan and West Coast of Patagonia made during the voyage of H.M.S. Nassau in the years 1866, 67, 68, and 69. Edinburgh, Edmonston and Douglas, 1871. xvi, 517 p. map, illus.

There is also some material on Rio de Janeiro.

99. DE BONELLI, L. Hugh

Travels in Bolivia; with a tour across the pampas to Buenos Ayres etc. 2 vols. London, Hurst and Blackett, 1854. 315; 328 p.

De Bonelli was a member of 'Her Britannic Majesty's Legation'.

100. ELWES, Robert

A sketcher's tour round the world. With illustrations from original drawings by the author. London, Hurst and Blackett, 1854. xii, 411 p. illus.

Contains material on Rio de Janeiro, Buenos Aires, Santiago, Valparaiso and Lima.

101. FITZROY, Robert (editor)

Narrative of the surveying voyages of His Majesty's Ships 'Adventure' and 'Beagle' between the years 1826 and 1836, describing their examination of the southern shores of South America, and the 'Beagle's' Circumnavigation of the globe. Volume 1. Proceedings of the first expedition, 1826–30 by Capt. P. Parker King. Volume 2. Proceedings of the Second expedition 1831–36 by Capt. Robert FitzRoy. Volume 3. Journal and remarks by Charles Darwin 1832–36. London, Henry Colburn, 1839. xxviii, 597; xiv, 694; xiv, 615 p. maps, illus.

Also an appendix to Volume 2: viii, 352 p. Colburn issued Darwin's volume as a separate work in the same year.

102. GARDINER, Allen Francis (Captain R.N.)

A Visit to the Indians on the frontiers of Chile. London, Seeley and Burnside, 1840. 194 p. map, illus.

After a career as a naval officer, Gardiner became a missionary and eventually died in an ill-fated expedition to the southern tip of South America. This item also contains material on Rio de Janeiro and the Río de la Plata. *Cf.* next item.

103. GARDINER, Allen Francis

A voice from South America. London, Seeley, Burnside and Seeley, 1847. iv, 107 p.

Not devoted to any specific region. *Cf.* previous item.

104. HADFIELD, William

Brazil, the River Plate and the Falkland Islands; with the Cape Horn route to Australia. Including notices of Lisbon, Madeira, the Canaries, and Cape Verds. London, Longman, Brown, Green and Longmans, 1854. vi, 384 p. map, illus.

Hadfield was many years resident in Brazil. He was at times secretary to the Buenos Aires Great Southern Railway and to the South American Steam Navigation Company, and editor of the *South American Journal. Cf.* items 105, 172 and 232.

105. HADFIELD, William

Brazil and the river Plate in 1868. London, Bates and Hendy, 1869. 271 p. illus.

'Showing the progress of those countries since his former visit in 1853'—Title-page. *Cf.* items 104, 172 and 232.

106. HINCHLIFF, Thomas Woodbine

South American sketches; or a visit to Rio Janeiro, the Organ mountains, La Plata, and the Parana. London, Longman, Green, Longman, Roberts and Green, 1863. xviii, 414 p. map, illus.

By profession a barrister, Hinchliff was a founder member and President of the Alpine Club. *Cf.* item 233.

107. JACKMAN, William

The Australian captive: or, an Authentic narrative of fifteen years in the life of William Jackman: in which, among various other adventures, is included a forced residence of a year and a half among the cannibals of Nuyts' Land, on the coast of the Great Australian Bight. Also including, with other appendices, Australia and its gold, from the latest and best authorities. Edited by Rev. I. Chamberlayne. London, Sampson Low, Auburn (U.S.A.), Derby and Miller, 1853. xvi, 392 p. illus.

Pages 262–343 include accounts of service in various ships round the South American coast, during the 1840's. There is some material on the Brazilian slave trade.

108. KENNEDY, A. J. (Commander R.N.)

La Plata, Brazil, and Paraguay, during the present war. London, Edward Stanford, 1869. viii, 273 p. map.

Kennedy commanded the gun-boat *Spider* which was patrolling in the area at the time.

109. MANSFIELD, Charles Blachford

Paraguay, Brazil and the Plate. Letters written in 1852–53. Cambridge, Macmillan, 1856. xxi, 504 p. map, front.

Mansfield was a chemist, but he had wide interests including social reform.

110. OUSELEY, William Gore (Sir)

Description of views in South America, from original

drawings, made in Brazil, the River Plate, the Parana etc etc. with notes. London, Thomas McLean, 1852. viii, 118 p.

Ouseley was a career diplomat who served in Brazil, Argentina and Central America.

111. REYNOLDS, Jeremiah N.

Voyage of the United States frigate Potomac, under the command of Commodore John Downes, during the circumnavigation of the globe, in the years 1831, 1832, 1833, and 1834; including a particular account of the engagement at Quallah-Battoo, on the coast of Sumatra; with all the official documents relating to the same. New York, Harper, 1835. x, 11–560 p. illus.

Includes a visit to Rio de Janeiro and an account of some west coast ports.

112. RICKARD, Francis Ignacio

A mining journey across the great Andes; with explorations in the silver mining districts of the provinces of San Juan and Mendoza, and a journey across the pampas to Buenos Ayres. London, Smith, Elder, 1863. xvi, 314 p. maps.

Cf. item 142.

113. RUSCHENBERGER, William Samuel Waithman

Three years in the Pacific; including notices of Brazil, Chile, Bolivia, and Peru. Philadelphia, Carey, Lea and Blanchard, 1834. xi, 441 p.

Published anonymously. Ruschenberger was a surgeon in the U.S. Navy.

114. SCARLETT, Peter Campbell (Honourable)

South America and the Pacific: comprising a journey across the pampas and the Andes, from Buenos Ayres to Valparaiso, Lima and Panama: with remarks upon the isthmus. To which are annexed plans and statements for establishing steam navigation on the Pacific. 2 vols. London, Henry Colburn, 1838. xii, 314; viii, 352 p. maps, illus.

Scarlett was a career diplomat. He was envoy extraordinary at Rio de Janeiro from 1855 to 1858.

115. SMYTH, William *and* LOWE, Frederick

Narrative of a journey from Lima to Para, across the Andes and down the Amazon: undertaken with a view of ascertaining the practicability of a navigable communication with the Atlantic, by the rivers Pachita, Ucayali, and Amazon. London, John Murray, 1836. vii, 305 p. maps, illus.

116. STANLEY, Edward Henry Smith (15th Earl of Derby)

Six weeks in South America. London, privately printed, 1850. iv, 132 p.

The book contains material on Colombia and Ecuador. The Earl of Derby subsequently served as Foreign Secretary under Disraeli (1874–78) and as Colonial Secretary under Gladstone (1882–85).

117. STEWART, Charles Samuel

Brazil and La Plata: the personal record of a cruise. New York, Putnam, 1856. xi, 428 p.

Stewart was chaplain on the *Congress. Cf.* item 21.

118. STRAIN, Isaac G.

Cordillera and pampa, mountain and plain. Sketches of a journey in Chili and the Argentine provinces in 1849. New York, Horace H. Moore, 1853. xi, 295 p.

Strain was a naval officer as well as an explorer. This trip was a private venture.

119. TAYLOR, Fitch Waterman

The flagship or a voyage round the world, and visits to various foreign countries, in the United States frigate Columbia; attended by her consort the sloop of war John Adams, and commanded by Commodore George C. Read. Also including an account of the bombarding and firing of the town of Muckie, on the Malay coast, and the visit of the ship to China during the opium difficulties at Canton, and confinement of the foreigners in that city. 2 vols. New York, D. Appleton, 1840. illus.

Taylor was a ship's chaplain. This work went through several editions in the 1840's. It contains accounts of Rio de Janeiro, Valparaiso, Santiago, Lima and Callao.

120. VIGNE, Godfrey Thomas

Travels in Mexico, South America, etc. etc. 2 vols. London, W. H. Allen, 1863. iv, 374; 317 p. map, illus.

Vigne was a barrister and was an enthusiastic traveller. This work includes material on the whole of South America. But its disjointed character reflects the fact that the author died leaving it incomplete.

121. WALPOLE, Fred (Lieutenant the Honourable, R.N.)

Four years in the Pacific. In Her Majesty's Ship 'Collingwood'. From 1844 to 1848. 2 vols. London, Richard Bentley, 1849. xiii, 432; ix, 415 p. illus.

Contains material on many parts of South America.

122. WARREN, Thomas Robinson

Dust and foam; or, three oceans and two continents being ten years wanderings in Mexico, South America, Sandwich Islands, East and West Indies, China, Philippines, Australia and Polynesia. New York, Charles Scribner, London, Sampson Low, 1859. xiii, 397 p. front.

The edition described is the second.

123. WILKES, Charles

Narrative of the United States exploring expedition during the years 1838, 1839, 1840, 1841, 1842. 5 vols. and an atlas. Philadelphia, C. Sherman, 1844. maps, illus.

Volume 1 (lxvi, 455 p.) contains descriptions of South America. The work went into several editions.

124. WILLIAMSON, John Gustavus Adolphus

Caracas diary 1835–40; the journal of John G. A. Williamson, first diplomatic representative of the United States to Venezuela. Edited by Jane Lucas de Grummond. Baton Rouge, La., Camellia Publishing Company, 1954. xxiv, 444 p.

(b) Río de la Plata Region

125. BISHOP, Nathaniel Holmes

The pampas and Andes. A thousand miles' walk across South America. Boston, Lee and Shepard, 1869. 310 p.

This item is principally about Argentina. The journey took place in 1854.

126. BOURNE, Benjamin Franklin
The captive in Patagonia: or life among the giants. A Personal narrative. Boston, Gould and Lincoln, 1853. 233 p. illus.

127. BURTON, Richard Francis
Letters from the battle-fields of Paraguay. London, Tinsley, 1870. xix, 491 p. map, illus.
An explorer and scholar, Burton's career was a mixture of research and high adventure. An intimate knowledge of Moslem manners and customs was crowned in 1853 by a pilgrimage in disguise to Mecca. He explored Somaliland and the sources of the Nile. A diplomatic career embraced appointments in Fernando Po, Santos (where he was British consul from 1865 to 1869), Damascus and Trieste. He was created K.C.M.G. in 1885. *Cf.* item 152.

128. CUSHING, S. W.
Wild oats sowings; or the autobiography of an adventurer. New York, Daniel Fanshaw, 1857. 483 p.
Cushing served with Garibaldi against Rosas.

129. HOPKINS, Edward Augustus
Historico-political memorial upon the regions of the Rio de la Plata, and conterminous countries, to James Buchanan, President of the United States. New York, Pudney and Russell for private circulation, 1858. 63 p. front.
Hopkins was United States special agent to Paraguay in 1846 and consul to the same country in 1854.

130. HUTCHINSON, Thomas Joseph
Buenos Ayres and Argentine gleanings: with extracts from a diary of Salado exploration in 1862 and 1863. London, Edward Stanford, 1865. xxi, 321 p. maps, illus.
Hutchinson was British consul at Rosario. *Cf.* items 131 and 300.

131. HUTCHINSON, Thomas Joseph

The Parana; with incidents of the Paraguayan war, and South American recollections, from 1861 to 1868. London, Edward Stanford, 1868. xxvii, 424 p. map, illus.

Cf. items 130 and 300.

131a. JOHNSON, Henry Charles Ross

A long vacation in the Argentine Alps or where to settle in the River Plate states. London, Richard Bentley, 1868. viii, 180 p. map.

132. LATHAM, Wilfrid

The states of the river Plate: their industries and commerce. Sheep-farming, sheep-breeding, cattle-feeding, and meat-preserving; employment of capital; land and stock, and their values; labour and its remuneration. London, Longmans, Green, 1866. vii, 200 p.

Latham lived for 24 years in the region. Longmans put out a more substantial second edition in 1868 (x, 381 p.).

133. MACCANN, William

Two thousand miles' ride through the Argentine provinces: being an account of the natural products of the country, and habits of the people; with a historical retrospect of the Rio de la Plata, Monte Video, and Corrientes. 2 vols. London, Smith, Elder, 1853. xiv, 295; x, 323 p. map, illus.

134. MCCOLL, John

The Republic of Uruguay, Monte Video, geographical, social, and industrial. A manual for emigrants to the River Plate. To which is appended, Life in the River Plate. London, Effingham Wilson, 1862. 72 p. maps, illus.

'By authority of the Monte Videan government.'—On title-page.

135. MACKINNON, Lauchlay Bellingham

Steam warfare in the Parana: a narrative of operations by the combined squadrons of England and France, in forcing a passage up that river. 2 vols. London, Charles Ollier, 1848. xii, 302; vii, 287 p. map.

136. MACRAE, Archibald

Report of journeys across the Andes and Pampas of the Argentine provinces. Washington, A. O. P. Nicholson, 1855. ix, 300 p.

Cf. item 185. This is the second volume of the report of that expedition. It does not carry a special title-page, though it is separately paginated. *Cf.* also 195.

137. MASTERMAN, George Frederick

Seven eventful years in Paraguay. A narrative of personal experience amongst the Paraguayans. London, Sampson Low and Marston, 1869. xv, 356 p.

Masterman was chief military apothecary for the Paraguayan forces during the Paraguayan war.

138. MULHALL, Michael George *and* MULHALL, Edward T.

Handbook of the River Plate; comprising Buenos Ayres, the Upper Provinces, Banda Oriental and Paraguay. Buenos Ayres, Standard Printing Office. maps.

The Mulhall brothers founded the *Buenos Ayres Standard*. The work described here was first published in 1863, but saw a number of editions during the rest of the century, for example in 1869, 1875 and 1892. *Cf.* item 281.

139. PAGE, Thomas Jefferson

La Plata, the Argentine confederation and Paraguay. Being a narrative of the exploration of the tributaries of the River La Plata and adjacent countries during the years 1853, '54, '55, and '56, under the orders of the United States Government. London, Trübner, 1859. xvi, 632 p. map, illus.

Page was a naval officer and explorer. He reached the rank of commander before his career was cut short when he fought on the Confederate side in the Civil War.

140. PARISH, Woodbine (Sir)

Buenos Ayres, and the provinces of Rio de la Plata: their

present state, trade, and debt; with some account from original documents of the progress of geographical discovery in those parts of South America during the last sixty years. London, John Murray, 1838. xxviii, 415 p. map, illus.

Parish was appointed first consul-general to Buenos Aires and sailed there aboard H.M.S. *Cambridge* (*cf.* item 17). By 1825, he had concluded the first treaty made with any of the new Spanish American states, and was appointed chargé d'affaires. He continued to further British interests in the area until 1832, when he was transferred. Parish also had scientific interests, being a Fellow of the Royal Society and of the Geological and Geographical Societies. A second edition (John Murray, 1852, xlii, 434 p.) is expanded chiefly with material on the earlier history of the area.

141. PEABODY, George Augustus

South American journals 1858–59 by George Augustus Peabody. Edited from the original manuscript by his friend John Charles Phillips. Salem, Mass., Peabody Museum, 1937. xvi, 209 p. map, illus.

'. . . expedition . . . undertaken purely as a sporting venture . . . no claim to be aiding science.'—Introduction, page xi. The journals deal mainly with the Río de la Plata area.

141a. PERKINS, William

The colonies of Santa-Fe. Their origin, progress and present condition, with general observations on emigration to the Argentine Republic. Being a series of articles written for the 'Ferro-Carril' of Rosario, augmented by fresh data and statistics. Rosario de Santa-Fe, printed at the office of the *Ferro-Carril*, 1864. 91 p.

142. RICKARD, Francis Ignacio

The mineral and other resources of the Argentine republic (La Plata) in 1869. London, Longmans, Green, 1870. 323 p.

Rickard was at this time Government Inspector General of Mines of the Argentine Republic. 'Published by special authority of the national government'—Title-page. *Cf.* item 112.

143. ROBERTSON, John Parish *and* ROBERTSON, William
     Parish

Letters on South America; comprising travels on the banks of
the Parana and Rio de la Plata. 3 vols. London, John Murray,
1843. xi, iv, 320; ix, 300; vii, 345 p.
The Robertsons were Scottish merchants. *Cf.* item 144.

144. ROBERTSON, John Parish *and* ROBERTSON, William
     Parish

Letters on Paraguay; comprising an account of a four years'
residence in that republic, under the government of the dictator
Francia. 3 vols. London, John Murray, 1838–39. xxvii, 359; x,
342; xvi, 400 p. illus.
Cf. item 143. Murray originally published the first two
volumes as a complete work. But in 1839 Volume 3 appeared
entitled 'Francia's reign of terror, being the continuation of
Letters on Paraguay . . . in 3 volumes.'

145. SEYMOUR, Richard Arthur

Pioneering in the pampas or the first four years of a settler's
experience in the La Plata camps. London, Longmans, Green,
1869. xi, 180 p. map.

146. SNOW, William Parker

A two years' cruise off Tierra del Fuego, the Falkland Islands,
Patagonia and in the River Plate: a narrative of life in the
southern seas. 2 vols. London, Longman, Brown, Green, Longmans and Roberts, 1857. xv, 376; viii, 368 p. maps, illus.
Snow commanded the missionary ship *Allen Gardiner*.

147. THOMPSON, George

The war in Paraguay. With a historical sketch of the country
and its people and notes upon the military engineering of the
war. London, Longmans, Green, 1869. x, 347 p. maps, front.

148. WASHBURN, Charles Ames

The history of Paraguay, with notes of personal observations,
and reminiscences of diplomacy under difficulties. 2 vols.

Boston, Lee and Shepard, New York, Lee, Shepard and Dillingham, 1871. xii, 571; xiv, 627 p. maps, illus.

Washburn was U.S. Minister Resident at Asunción 1861 to 1868.

149. WHITTLE, W.

Journal of a voyage to the River Plate; including observations made during a residence in the republic of Montevideo. Manchester, Bradshaw and Blacklock, 1846. 102 p. front.

(c) Brazil

150. AGASSIZ, Elizabeth Cabot Cary *and* AGASSIZ, Jean Louis Rodolphe

A journey in Brazil. Boston, Ticknor and Fields, 1868. xix, 540 p. illus.

Born in French Switzerland, Agassiz had already made outstanding contributions to palaeontology, being particularly noted for his investigations of glacial phenomena, when in 1846 he emigrated to the United States. There he quickly established himself as the outstanding student of natural history. He took out American citizenship at the outbreak of the Civil War. His visit to Brazil represented for Agassiz the achievement of a long-held ambition. This account of the journey is largely written by his wife, but contains material by Agassiz himself.

151. BATES, Henry Walter

The naturalist on the river Amazons, a record of adventures, habits of animals, sketches of Brazilian and Indian life, and aspects of nature under the equator, during eleven years of travel. 2 vols. London, John Murray, 1863. ix, 351; vi, 423 p. maps, illus.

Bates was largely self-taught. He went with A. R. Wallace (*cf.* item 170) to Pará in 1848. His researches brought to light more than 8,000 species new to science. An Assistant Secretary of the Royal Geographical Society from 1864 to 1892, he was elected a Fellow of the Royal Society in 1881 and was President of the Entomological Society in 1869 and 1878. *Cf.* item 212.

152. BURTON, Richard Francis

Explorations of the highlands of Brazil; with a full account of the gold and diamond mines. Also, canoeing down 1500 miles of the great river São Francisco, from Sabara to the sea. 2 vols. London, Tinsley, 1869. xii, 443; viii, 478 p.

This is sometimes short-titled: The highlands of Brazil. *Cf.* item 127.

153. CANDLER, John *and* BURGESS, Wilson

Narrative of a recent visit to Brazil; to present an address on the slave-trade and slavery, issued by the Religious Society of Friends. London, Friends' Book and Tract Depository, 1853. 91 p.

154. CHRISTIE, William Dougal

Notes on Brazilian questions. London, Macmillan, 1865. lxxi, 236 p.

Christie was called to the bar in 1840, and was a member of the House of Commons from 1842 to 1847. In 1848, he entered the diplomatic service, and was envoy extraordinary and minister plenipotentiary to Brazil 1859–63. His retirement was devoted to writing, mainly on literary and historical topics.

155. CODMAN, John

Ten months in Brazil: with incidents of voyages and travels, descriptions of scenery and character, notices of commerce and productions, etc. Boston, Lee and Shepard, 1867. 208 p. illus.

156. DUNDAS, Robert

Sketches of Brazil; including new views on tropical and European fever, with remarks on a premature decay of the system incident to Europeans on their return from hot climates. London, John Churchill, 1852. x, 449 p.

157. DUNN, Ballard S.

Brazil, the home for southerners: or a practical account of what the author, and others, who visited that country for the same objects, saw and did while in that empire. New York,

George B. Richardson, New Orleans, Bloomfield and Steel, 1866. 272, [23] p. front.

158. EDWARDS, William Henry

A voyage up the river Amazon, including a residence at Para. New York, D. Appleton, Philadelphia, G. S. Appleton, 1847. 256 p. front.

Edwards was an entomologist.

159. EWBANK, Thomas

Life in Brazil; or, A journal of a visit to the land of the cocoa and the palm. With an appendix containing illustrations of ancient South American arts in recently discovered implements and products of domestic industry, and works in stone, pottery, gold, silver, bronze, etc. New York, Harper, 1856. xiv, 17–469 p. illus.

Ewbank was an inventor and manufacturer. He was U.S. Commissioner of Patents 1849–52. His book describes Rio de Janeiro and its surroundings.

160. FLETCHER, James Cooley and KIDDER, Daniel Parish

Brazil and the Brazilians, portrayed in historical and descriptive sketches. Philadelphia, Childs and Peterson, 1857. 630 p. map, illus.

Fletcher and Kidder were Methodist missionaries. Kidder worked in Brazil from 1837 to 1840. Fletcher worked at the United States legation in Rio de Janeiro in 1852 and subsequently had several spells of work in Brazil as a missionary. *Cf.* item 164.

161. GARDNER, George

Travels in the interior of Brazil, principally through the northern provinces, and the gold and diamond districts during the years 1836–41. London, Reeve, 1846. xvi, 562 p. map, front.

Gardner was a botanist who attained the post of superintendent of the Royal Botanic Gardens, Ceylon.

162. HERNDON, William Lewis and GIBBON, Lardner

Exploration of the valley of the Amazon, made under direction of the Navy Department. Part I by Lieut. Herndon. Part

II by Lt. Lardner Gibbon. 2 vols. Washington, Robert Armstrong, 1853. 414, iv; x, 339 p. illus.

This was originally published as a government document but was also put out as an independent publication by the government printer. It contains material on Chile and Bolivia as well as on the Amazon. Volume 2 of the independently published edition appeared under the imprint of A. O. P. Nicholson.

163. JOHNSON, Daniel Noble

The journals of Daniel Noble Johnson (1822–63) United States Navy. Edited by Mendel L. Peterson. Washington, Smithsonian Institution, 1959. iv, 268 p. illus. (Smithsonian Miscellaneous Collections, Vol. 136, No. 2.)

The author entitled his two accounts: *Journal of a cruise on the Brazils on board of the U.S. Ship Delaware, 1841–42* and *Notes by the way while on board the U.S. Schooner Enterprise.*

164. KIDDER, Daniel Parish

Sketches of residence and travels in Brazil, embracing historical and geographical notices of the empire and its several provinces. 2 vols. London, Wiley and Putnam, Philadelphia, Sorin and Ball, 1845. xv, 369; vii, 404 p. illus.

Cf. item 160.

165. MARJORIBANKS, Alexander

Travels in South and North America. London, Simpkin, Marshall, New York, D. Appleton, 1853. xiv, 480 p. front, illus.

Deals predominantly with Brazil.

166. PATON, Alexander

Narrative of the Loss of the Schooner Clio, of Montrose, Captain George Reid; containing an account of the Massacre of her Crew by the Indians, on the North Coast of Brazil, in October, 1835; with other interesting particulars relative to the ... Adventures, and miraculous Escape of the Author from the hands of a Savage People. By Alexander Paton, a native of Ferryden, the only Survivor. Montrose, Smith, 1838, 60 p.

'Second edition, enlarged and improved.' The entry is taken from Sabin (59070).

167. PAYNE, A. R. Middletoun

The Geral-Milco; or the Narrative of a Residence in a Brazilian valley of the Sierra Paricis. New York, Charles B. Norton, 1852. xii, 264 p. map, illus.

Jones (*South America Rediscovered*) says that this is pure fantasy. It describes the discovery of a tribe of Indians in Brazil.

168. SCULLY, William

Brazil; its provinces and chief cities; the manners and customs of the people; agricultural, commercial and other statistics, taken from the Latest Official Documents; with a variety of useful and entertaining knowledge, both for the merchant and the emigrant. London, Murray, 1866. xv, 398 p. map.

Scully was editor of the *Anglo-Brazilian Times*.

169. SPRUCE, Richard

Notes of a botanist on the Amazon and the Andes, being records of travel on the Amazon and its tributaries, the Trombetas, Rio Negro, Uaupes, Casiquiari, Pacimoni, Huallaga, and Pastasa; as also to the cataracts of the Orinoco, along the Eastern side of the Andes of Peru and Ecuador, and the shores of the Pacific, during the years 1849–64. Edited and condensed by Alfred Russel Wallace, with a biographical introduction, portrait, seventy-one illustrations and seven maps. 2 vols. London, Macmillan, 1908, lii, 518; xii, 542 p.

A botanist and traveller, Spruce was in South America between 1849 and 1864. It was in the Amazon region that he met Wallace. *Cf.* next item.

170. WALLACE, Alfred Russel

A narrative of travels on the Amazon and Rio Negro, with an account of the native tribes, and observations on the climate, geology, and natural history of the Amazon valley. London, Reeve, 1853. viii, 541 p. map, illus.

Wallace, like Bates (items 151 and 212), was a largely self-educated naturalist. His joint paper with Darwin to the Linnaean Society in 1858 launched the theory of evolution by natural selection. The *Dictionary of National Biography* describes

him as 'an indefatigable collector, both of specimens and facts'.
A further edition was published in 1889.

171. WARREN, John Esaias
   Para; or, scenes and adventures on the banks of the Amazon.
New York, G. P. Putnam, 1851. 271 p.

172. WETHERELL, James
   Brazil. Stray notes from Bahia: being extracts from letters,
etc. during a residence of fifteen years. Edited by William
Hadfield. Liverpool, Webb and Hunt, 1860. viii, 153 p. front.
   Cf. items 104, 105 and 232.

173. WILBERFORCE, Edward
   Brazil viewed through a naval glass: with notes on slavery and
the slave trade. London, Longman, Brown, Green and Long-
mans, 1856. x, 126, 127–236 p.
   Issued in two continuously paginated parts in the *Traveller's
Library* series.

(d) West Coast

174. BAXLEY, Henry Willis
   What I saw on the West Coast of South and North America,
and at the Hawaiian Islands. New York, D. Appleton, 1865.
632 p. illus.
   Baxley was a physician and surgeon. His trip was basically a
mission to reform hospital work under consular supervision.
The book contains material on Peru, Chile and Ecuador.

175. BEALE, Thomas
   The natural history of the sperm whale: its anatomy and
physiology—food—spermaceti—ambergris—rise and progress of
the fishery—chase and capture—'cutting in' and 'trying out'—
description of the ship, boats, men, and instruments used in the
attack; with an account of its favourite places of resort. To
which is added a sketch of a south-sea whaling voyage; embracing a description of the extent, as well as the adventures and

accidents that occurred during the voyage in which the author was personally engaged. London, John Van Voorst, 1839. 12, 393 p. illus.

This contains material on Peru, and on Tierra del Fuego and Patagonia. In 1835, Beale published *A few observations on the natural history of the sperm whale* (London, Effingham Wilson, 58 p.). It contains no material on South America.

176. BROWN, Charles H.

Insurrection at Magellan. Narrative of the imprisonment and escape of Capt. Chas. H. Brown, from the Chilian convicts. Boston, Geo. C. Rand for the author, 1854. 228 p. front.

177. BYAM, George

Wanderings in some of the western republics of America. With remarks upon the cutting of the great ship canal through Central America. London, John Parker, 1850. xii, 264 p. map, plates.

178. CARLETON, George Washington

Our artist in Peru. Leaves from the sketch book of a traveller, during the winter of 1865–6. New York, Carleton, London, Sampson Low, 1866. viii, 50 p.

Consists of 50 sketches.

179. CARVELL, Henry de Wolfe

Insecurity of British property in Peru. Imprisonment of a British subject. Contempt of British authority. Bad faith and fraud in the administration of the law. Persecution endured in the attempt to obtain justice. An appeal to the representatives of the British nation by Henry de Wolfe Carvell. London, Chapman and Hall, 1863. xii, 70 p.

180. CORNWALLIS, Kinahan

A panorama of the New World. 2 vols. London, T. C. Newby, 1859. viii, 430; 300 p.

Though Cornwallis writes principally about Australia, Volume 2 of his book contains material on Peru and Chile.

181. COULTER, John

Adventures in the Pacific; with observations on the natural productions, manners and customs of the natives of the various islands; together with remarks on missionaries, British and other residents, etc. etc. Dublin, William Curry Junior, London, Longmans, Brown, Edinburgh, Fraser, 1845. xi, 290 p.

Contains some material on Chile. *Cf.* item 182.

182. COULTER, John

Adventures on the Western coast of South America, and the interior of California: including a narrative of incidents at the Kingsmill Islands, New Ireland, New Britain, New Guinea, and other islands in the Pacific Ocean; with an account of the natural productions, and the manners and customs, in peace and war, of the various savage tribes visited. 2 vols. London, Longman, Brown, Green and Longmans, 1847. xxiv, 288; xii, 278 p.

Cf. item 181.

183. A DIARY OF THE WRECK of His Majesty's Ship Challenger, on the Western coast of South America, in May, 1835. With an account of the subsequent encampment of the officers and crew, during a period of seven weeks, on the South coast of Chili. London, Longman, Rees, Orme, Brown, Green and Longman, 1836. 160 p. map. illus.

The diary is by one of the ship's officers, possibly Lieutenant G. A. Rothery.

184. DUFFY, James William (Doctor)

A hand-book to Valparaiso containing the laws and regulations of the port, expenses incurred by ships upon their arrival, and general information useful to masters of British and American vessels, and others, conversant with the English language; to which is added a brief description of the town, and a chronological table of the principal events in the history of Chile. Valparaiso, W. Hefmann's 'Universe' Printing Office, 1862. viii, 64 p. plan.

Published anonymously.

185. GILLISS, James Melville

Chile: its geography, climate, earthquakes, government, social condition, mineral and agricultural resources etc. etc. Washington, A. O. P. Nicholson, 1855. xiii, 556 p. maps, illus. *Cf.* item 136.

This constitutes Volume 1 of 'The U.S. Naval Astronomical Expedition to the Southern Hemisphere during the years 1849-'50-'51-'52'. It was published as an official government publication. Gilliss later became head of the U.S. Naval Observatory. *Cf.* item 195.

186. HASSAUREK, Friedrich

Four years among Spanish-Americans. New York, Hurd and Houghton, 1868. x, 401 p.

'Late U.S. minister resident to the Republic of Ecuador'— Title-page.

187. HILL, S. S.

Travels in Peru and Mexico. 2 vols. London, Longman, Green, Longman, and Roberts, 1860. xiii, 330; xii, 312 p.

Hill also wrote travel books on other regions. This one also contains material on Chile.

188. MARKHAM, Clements Robert (Sir)

Cuzco: a journey to the ancient capital of Peru; with an account of the history, language, literature, and antiquities of the Incas. And Lima: a visit to the capital and provinces of modern Peru; with a sketch of the viceregal government, history of the republic, and a review of the literature and society of Peru. London, Chapman and Hall, 1856. iv, 412 p. map, illus.

Markham served in both the navy and the civil service. From 1867 to 1877, he was in charge of geographical work at the India Office. In 1873 he was elected a Fellow of the Royal Society. He accompanied the Arctic expedition of Sir G. S. Nares in 1875 and was a promoter of Antarctic exploration. He was at times President of the Hakluyt Society and of the Royal Geographical Society and was made a K.C.B. in 1896. *Cf.* items 189 and 302.

189. MARKHAM, Clements Robert (Sir)

Travels in Peru and India while superintending the collection of Chinchona plants and seeds in South America, and their introduction into India. London, John Murray, 1862. xviii, 572 p. maps, illus.

Cf. items 188 and 302.

190. MERWIN, C. B. (Mrs.)

Three years in Chili. New York, Follett and Foster, 1863. viii, 158 p.

Mrs. Merwin's husband was U.S. consul in Valparaiso. The book was published anonymously.

191. PECK, George Washington

Melbourne, and the Chincha islands; with sketches of Lima, and a voyage round the World. New York, Charles Scribner, 1854. v, 13–294 p. maps, illus.

Peck was an author, journalist and music critic. Pages 141–284 of his book relate to South America, especially Callao and Lima.

192. PRINCE, George

Rambles in Chile, and life among the Araucanian Indians, in 1836. By Will the Rover. Thomaston, D. J. Starrett, 1851. iv, 9–88 p.

Prince's name does not appear on the title-page.

193. RECOLLECTIONS OF A RAMBLE from Sydney to Southampton; viâ South America, Panama, the West Indies, the United States, and Niagara. London, Richard Bentley, 1851. viii, 340 p.

The first 150 pages relate to Chile and Peru.

194. SMITH, Archibald

Peru as it is: a residence in Lima, and other parts of the Peruvian republic, comprising an account of the social and physical features of that country. 2 vols. London, Richard Bentley, 1839. xi, 299; v, 308 p.

195. SMITH, Edmond Reuel

The Araucanians; or, Notes of a tour among the Indian tribes of Southern Chili. New York, Harper, 1855. xii, 335 p. illus.

Smith was a member of the U.S. Naval Astronomical Expedition of 1849–52.

Cf. items 136 and 185.

196. TERRY, Adrian Russell

Travels in the equatorial regions of South America in 1832. Hartford, Cooke, 1834. 290 p. front.

Contains material on Ecuador.

197. WEBBER, Vivian Arthur

Journal of a voyage round Cape Horn. Swansea, printed by W. M. Bruster, 1859. vii, 163 p.

Some information about Chile.

198. WHITE, T. Melville (Captain)

Britons robbed, tortured and murdered in Peru. London, for the author, 1862. xi, 144 p.

199. WISE, Henry Augustus (Lieutenant U.S.N.)

Los gringos: or an inside view of Mexico and California, with wanderings in Peru, Chili, and Polynesia. London, Richard Bentley, 1849. xvi, 406 p.

Published simultaneously by Baker and Scribner in New York (xvi, 453 p.). The book also contains a description of Rio de Janeiro.

(e) North

200. BROMLEY, Clara Fitzroy (Mrs.)

A woman's wanderings in the Western world. A series of letters addressed to Sir Fitzroy Kelly M.P. by his daughter. London, Saunders and Otley, 1861. 299 p. illus.

Contains material on the north of South America.

201. EASTWICK, Edward Backhouse

Venezuela; sketches of life in a South-American republic; with the history of the loan of 1864. London, Chapman and Hall, 1868. xi, 418 p. map.

Eastwick was a diplomat. He was commissioner for the Venezuelan loan.

202. EMPSON, Charles

Narratives of South America; illustrating manners, customs, and scenery: containing also numerous facts in natural history, collected during a four years' residence in tropical regions. London, William Edwards for the author, 1836. xvi, 322 p.

Principally Colombia.

203. HAWKSHAW, John (Sir)

Reminiscences of South America: from two and a half years' residence in Venezuela. London, Jackson and Walford, 1838. xii, 260 p.

204. HOLTON, Isaac Farwell

New Granada: twenty months in the Andes. New York, Harper, 1857. xiv, 605 p. maps. illus.

205. STEUART, John

Bogota in 1836–7. Being a narrative of an expedition to the Capital of New-Grenada, and a residence there of eleven months. New York, Harper for the author, 1838. viii, 312 p.

206. SULLIVAN, Edward Robert (Sir)

Rambles and scrambles in North and South America. London, Richard Bentley, 1852. viii, 424 p.

A description of Venezuela pages 300 to 400.

III. 1870–1900

(a) General

207. AKERS, Charles Edmond

Argentine, Patagonian and Chilean sketches with a few notes on Uruguay. London, Harrison, 1893. 190 p.

Akers was a correspondent for *The Times*.

208. ALCOCK, Frederick

Trade and travel in South America. London, George Philip, 1903. xix, 573 p. maps, illus.

'. . . the story of my travels round South America . . .'—Page 2. The travel account is mingled with straightforward commercial intelligence. It is not made clear whether the journey took place before the turn of the century.

209. ATCHISON, Charles C.

A winter cruise in summer seas. How I found health. Diary of a two months' voyage in the Royal Mail Steam Packet Company's s.s. Clyde, from Southampton, through the Brazils, to Buenos Aires and back for £100. London, Sampson Low, Marston, 1891. xxx, 369 p. illus.

210. BALL, John

Notes of a naturalist in South America. London, Kegan Paul, Trench, 1887. xiii, 416 p. map.

A scientist and politician, Ball was at one time President of the Alpine Club, and also served as Under-Secretary for the Colonies from 1855 to 1857. His book has material on the whole of South America.

211. BALLOU, Maturin Murray

Equatorial America, descriptive of a visit to St. Thomas, Martinique, Barbados, and the principal capitals of South America. Boston, New York, Houghton, Mifflin, 1892. x, 371 p.

Ballou was a professional journalist and writer. He was first editor and manager of the *Boston Daily Globe*.

212. BATES, Henry Walter

Central America, the West Indies and South America. London, 1878. xviii, 571 p. maps, illus.

This was published by Edward Stanford in the series *Stanford's Compendium of Geography and Travel*. It was based to some extent on Hellwald's *Die Erde und Ihre Volker* though revisions and extensions reflect Bates's own acquaintanceship with the area. The book saw several editions. *Cf.* item 151.

213. BRASSEY, Annie (Baroness)

A voyage in the 'Sunbeam'. Our home on the ocean for 11 months. London, Longmans, Green, 1878. xv, 504 p. maps, illus.

Lady Brassey's maiden name was Allnutt. The New York edition (published by Holt) was entitled *Around the world in the yacht 'Sunbeam', our home on the ocean for 11 months*. Pages 46–194 of the edition noted contain accounts of Rio de Janeiro, Argentina and Chile.

214. CARLISLE, Arthur Drummond

Round the world in 1870: an account of a brief tour made through India, China, Japan, California and South America. London, Henry S. King, 1872. xii, 408 p.

Descriptions of South America occupy pages 283 to 400.

215. CARPENTER, Frank George

South America: social, industrial and political. A twenty-five-thousand-mile journey in search of information in the Isthmus of Panama and the lands of the Equator, Colombia, Ecuador, Peru, Bolivia, Chile, Tierra del Fuego, the Falklands, Argentina, Paraguay, Uruguay, Brazil, the Guianas, Venezuela, and the Orinoco Basin. The resources and possibilities of the various countries—the life and customs of the people—their governments, business methods, and trade. Akron, Ohio, Saalfield Publishing Company, 1900. 625 p.

'The journey occupied about a year of constant travel, during which the author visited the various countries spending some time in their capitals and ports, and making many journeys into the interior.'—Author's preface. Carpenter was a prolific traveller and writers. He used to say that his books were intended 'for ordinary people like myself'.

216. CATLIN, George

Last rambles amongst the Indians of the Rocky Mountains and the Andes. London, Sampson Low and Marston, 1868. x, 361 p. illus.

D. Appleton of New York published the first American edition in 1867.

Catlin was an artist who devoted his life to Indian portraiture. His book contains material on Rio de Janeiro, Buenos Aires and Tierra del Fuego, pages 206 to 304.

217. CHILD, Theodore

The Spanish-American republics. New York, Harper, 1891. xii, 444 p. maps, illus.

'A plain narrative of observation and travel in the more accessible parts of the five important republics of Spanish South America, Chili, Peru, the Argentine, Paraguay and Uruguay . . .'—Author's preface.

218. CONWAY, William Martin (Sir)

Aconcagua and Tierra del Fuego. A book of climbing, travel and exploration. London etc., Cassell, 1902. xii, 252 p.

The climb took place in December 1898. *Cf.* item 294.

219. COPPINGER, Richard William

Cruise of the 'Alert'. Four years in Patagonian, Polynesian and Mascarene waters, 1878–82. London, W. Swan Sonnenschein, 1883. xiii, 256 p. illus.

Coppinger was ship's surgeon but also an amateur naturalist. He later became Inspector-General of Hospitals and Fleets. His book contains material on Patagonia and Chile, and on the war between Chile, Peru and Bolivia.

220. CRAWFORD, Robert

Across the pampas and the Andes. London, Longmans, Green, 1884. xxii, 344 p. map, illus.

Crawford was an engineer engaged in surveying the route of the proposed Trans-Andine Railway for Warings of London and the 'Government of Buenos Ayres'. He describes the Río de la Plata region and Chile. *Cf.* items 250 and 251.

221. CROMMELIN, Maria Henrietta de la Cherois

Over the Andes from the Argentine to Chile and Peru. London, Richard Bentley, 1896. viii, 387 p. illus.

222. CURTIS, William Eleroy

The capitals of Spanish America. New York, Harper, 1888. xv, 715 p. map, illus.

Curtis served as U.S. government commissioner to the governments of South and Central America. He was later the first director of the Bureau of the American Republics (1889–93) which became the Pan American Union. *Cf.* items 295 and 312.

223. DEWAR, James Cumming

Voyage of the 'Nyanza' R.N.Y.C. being a record of a three years' cruise in a schooner yacht in the Atlantic and Pacific, and her subsequent shipwreck. Edinburgh and London, William Blackwood, 1892. xviii, 466 p. map, illus.

Pages 1 to 153 contain material on Rio de Janeiro, the River Plate, Valparaiso and Peru.

224. DICKINS, Marguerite

Along shore with a man-of-war. Boston, Arena Publishing Company, 1893. 242 p. illus.

'For two years and a half I sailed up and down the east coast of South America . . .'—Author's introduction.

225. DINGMAN, Benjamin S.

Ten years in South America. Notes of travel in Peru, Bolivia, Chile, Argentine Republic, Montevideo and Brazil, comprising history, commercial statistics, climate, products etc. Montreal, Gazette Printing House, 1876.

'Part Second: Bolivia complete in itself' was certainly published and itself confirms the publication of the account of Peru. The author suggests in 'Part Second' that publication of the remainder depends to some extent on public approbation, and concludes the part by stating 'The third part, entitled Chile, will immediately follow.' I found no trace of this part.

226. DUFFIELD, Alexander James

Recollections of travels abroad. London, Remington, 1889. xiv, 327 p. map.

Duffield worked as a mining chemist in Peru and Bolivia. *Cf.* items 297 and 298.

227. EDGECUMBE, Edward Robert Pearce-

Zephyrus; a holiday in Brazil and on the River Plate. London, Chatto and Windus, 1887. 242 p. map, illus.

228. EVANS, Patrick Fleming

From Peru to the Plate, overland. London, Bates and Hendy, 1889. 124 p. map.

Evans travelled via Bolivia.

229. FORD, Isaac Nelson

Tropical America. New York, Charles Scribner, 1893. x, 409 p. map, illus.

Ford travelled widely throughout South America.

230. FOUNTAIN, Paul

The great mountains and forests of South America. London, New York, Longmans, Green, 1902. 306 p. illus.

'It was in the year 1884 that I first saw the southern half of America, and I went straight to Brazil.'—Page 4. In fact, the book contains material on the entire continent.

231. GALLENGA, Antonio Carlo Napoleone

South America. London, Chapman and Hall, 1880. xi, 400 p. map.

Of Italian birth, Gallenga took British nationality in 1846. Based on a tour he made, his book contains material on all areas of South America.

232. HADFIELD, William

Brazil and the River Plate 1870–76. Sutton, Surrey, W. R. Church, London, Edward Stanford, 1877. 7, 327 p. illus.

'With supplement'—Note on title-page. *Cf.* items 104, 105 and 172.

233. HINCHLIFF, Thomas Woodbine

Over the sea and far away: being a narrative of wanderings round the world. London, Longmans, Green, 1876. xiv, 416 p. illus.

This book contains material on Rio de Janeiro, Buenos Aires, Santiago and Lima. *Cf.* item 106.

234. KENNEDY, William Robert (Admiral R.N.)

Sporting sketches in South America. London, R. H. Porter, 1892. xvi, 269 p. map, illus.

Principally Brazil and the Río de la Plata. *Cf.* item 301.

235. KNIGHT, Edward Frederick

The Cruise of the 'Falcon'. A voyage to South America in a 30-ton yacht. 2 vols. London, Sampson Low, Marston, Searle and Rivington, 1884. vi, 301; vi, 304 p. maps, illus.

'The narrative includes the description of five months' cruise in a yacht up the Rivers Parana and Paraguay, and of a ride across the Pampas to Tucuman.'—Author's preface.

236. LAMBERT, Charles J. *and* LAMBERT, S. (Mrs.)

The voyage of the 'Wanderer'. From the journals and letters of C. and S. Lambert. Edited by Gerald Young. London, Macmillan, 1883. xx, 335 p. map, illus.

In the first half of the book, there are descriptions of visits to a number of South American ports (Rio de Janeiro, Montevideo, Valparaiso) before the *Wanderer* headed out into the Pacific. The basis of the text is Charles Lambert's diary and his wife's letters.

237. MORANT, George C.

Chile and the river Plate in 1891. Reminiscences of travel in South America. London, Waterlow, 1891. 268 p. illus.

238. MULHALL, Marion McMurrough (Mrs.)

Between the Amazon and the Andes, or ten years of a lady's travels in the pampas, Gran Chaco, Paraguay, and Matto Grosso. London, Edward Stanford, 1881. xi, 340 p. maps, illus.
Cf. item 239.

239. MULHALL, Marion McMurrough (Mrs.)

From Europe to Paraguay and Matto-Grosso. London, Edward Stanford, 1877. 116 p. map, illus.
Cf. item 238.

240. MYERS, Henry Morris *and* MYERS, Philip Van Ness

Life and nature under the tropics; or, Sketches of travels among the Andes, and on the Orinoco, Rio Negro, Amazons, and in Central America. New York, D. Appleton, 1871. xvi, 358 p. map, illus.

241. ORTON, James

The Andes and the Amazon; or, across the continent of South America. New York, Harper, 1870. 356 p. map, illus.

Principally Ecuador and Brazil. A zoologist, explorer and educator, Orton was also ordained in the Presbyterian ministry. In 1869 he was appointed Professor of Natural History at Vassar.

242. SCRUGGS, William Lindsay

The Colombian and Venezuelan republics: with Notes on Other Parts of Central and South America. London, Sampson Low, Marston, Boston, Little, Brown, 1900. xii, 350 p. maps, illus.

'Late envoy extraordinary and minister plenipotentiary of the United States to Colombia and to Venezuela.'—Title-page.
'. . . a brief account of the author's personal experiences . . . more particularly in the republics of Colombia and Venezuela . . . from 1872 to 1899.'—Introduction.

Scruggs served in Colombia 1873–76 and 1882–85, and in Venezuela 1889–93. He supported Venezuela in her dispute with the British Government over the boundaries of British

Guiana, and in 1894 was appointed Venezuela's legal adviser and special agent in the matter.

243. VINCENT, Ethel Gwendoline

China to Peru, over the Andes. A journey through South America. By Mrs. Howard Vincent. With reports and letters on British interests in Brazil, Argentina, Chili, Peru, Panama and Venezuela by Col. Howard Vincent. London, Sampson Low, Marston, 1894. x, 333 p. maps, illus.

Vincent himself was a Member of Parliament.

244. VINCENT, Frank

Around and about South America: twenty months of quest and query. New York, D. Appleton, 1890. xxiv, 473 p. maps, illus.

'My recent journey through South America included visits to all the capitals, chief cities and important sea ports; expeditions into the interior of Brazil and the Argentine Republic; and ascents of the Parana, Paraguay, Amazon, Orinoco and Magdalena rivers.'

(b) Río de la Plata Region

245. BEERBOHM, Julius

Wanderings in Patagonia, or life among the ostrich-hunters. London, Chatto and Windus, 1879. 278 p. map. illus.

Further editions were published later.

246. CAMPBELL, W. O.

Through Patagonia. London, Bickers, 1901. viii, 96 p. map.

'I . . . have myself spent much time wandering in Patagonia.' —Author's preface.

247. CLARK, Edwin

A visit to South America; with notes and observations on the moral and physical features of the country, and the incidents of the voyage. London, Dean, 1878. 355 p. illus., tables.

'. . . notes made in 1876 and 1877, during a journey to the River Plate and a residence of nearly two years in Buenos Ayres, Paraguay, and Uruguay.'—Author's preface.

248. CLEMENS, Eliza Jane McCartney

La Plata countries of South America. Philadelphia, J. B. Lippincott, 1886. 511 p. map.

A particular feature of this book is the interest shown by the author in missionary activities.

249. COAN, Titus

Adventures in Patagonia, a missionary's exploring trip. New York, Dodd and Mead, 1880. 319 p. map.

250. CRAWFORD, Robert

Reminiscences of foreign travel. London, Longmans, Green, 1888. xx, 308 p.

Pages 166 to 224 describe a visit to the Río de la Plata. The contents include some material on Rosas. *Cf.* items 220 and 251.

251. CRAWFORD, Robert

South American sketches. London, Longmans, Green, 1898. xx, 280 p.

'This volume had its origin ... in a residence in Uruguay for three and a half years.' Whilst predominantly concerned with Uruguay, the author's attention is 'not ... exclusively confined within the limits of that republic'. *Cf.* items 220 and 250.

252. DARBYSHIRE, Charles

My life in the Argentine republic. London, New York, Frederick Warne, 1918. xii, 140 p. illus.

'In writing this little book my object has been, partly to show the condition of the Argentine Republic in 1852, when I first landed there, and also to show the progress the country had made when I paid my last visit in 1893–1894.'—Author's preface.

253. DIXIE, Florence Caroline (Lady)

Across Patagonia. London, Richard Bentley, 1880. xiii, 251 p. illus.

Lady Dixie (*née* Douglas) was the wife of Sir Alexander Beaumont Churchill Dixie.

254. DOBSON, Arthur Austin Greaves

A short account of the Leach Bermejo expedition of 1899, with some reference to the flora, fauna and Indian tribes of the Chaco. Buenos Aires, J. Smart, 1900. 74 p. illus.

Dobson was a correspondent of the *River Plate Sport and Pastime Magazine*.

255. FITZGERALD, Edward Arthur

The highest Andes. A record of the first ascent of Aconcagua and Tupungato in Argentina, and the exploration of the surrounding valleys. London, Methuen, 1899. xvi, 390 p. maps, illus.

'. . . the outcome of seven months work by myself and my colleagues, Mr. Stuart Vines, Mr. Arthur Lightbody and Mr. Philip Gosse, in the Andes of Argentina . . .'—Author's preface.

256. GIBSON, Herbert

The history and present state of the sheep-breeding industry in the Argentine republic. Buenos Aires, Ravenscroft and Mills, 1893. x, 297 p. maps, illus.

The book was aimed at prospective immigrants.

257. HUDSON, William Henry

Idle days in Patagonia. London, Chapman and Hall, 1893. vi, 256 p. illus.

Hudson was born and spent his early years, described in his autobiography *Far Away and Long Ago* (1918), in the Río de la Plata area. A severe illness in his youth permanently impaired his health, though he lived to 81. Travelling to England in 1869, he took many years to establish his reputation as a writer. In 1901 he was awarded a civil list pension. *Cf.* items 258 and 259.

258. HUDSON, William Henry

The naturalist in La Plata. London, Chapman and Hall, 1892. vii, 388 p. illus.

Cf. items 257 and 259.

259. HUDSON, William Henry

The purple land that England lost. Travels and adventures in the Banda Oriental, South America. 2 vols. London, Sampson Low, Marston, Searle and Rivington, 1885. iv, 286; iv, 265 p. This work, of course, went into many editions. Cf. items 257 and 258.

260. MURRAY, John Hall

Travels in Uruguay, South America; together with an account of the present state of sheep-farming and emigration to that country. London, Longmans and E. Stanford, 1871. viii, 234 p. illus.

261. MUSTERS, George Chaworth (Commander R.N.)

At home with the Patagonians. A year's wanderings over untrodden ground from the Straits of Magellan to the Rio Negro. London, John Murray, 1871. xii, 322 p. map, illus.

262. PELLESCHI, Giovanni

Eight months on the Gran Chaco of the Argentine Republic. London, Sampson Low, Marston, Searle and Rivington, 1886. xv, 311 p.

263. RUMBOLD, Horace (Sir)

The great silver river; notes of a residence in Buenos Ayres in 1880 and 1881. London, John Murray, 1887. 14, 330 p.

Privately educated, Rumbold entered the diplomatic service in 1849 as the nominee of Lord Palmerston. For much of his career, he failed to obtain the preferment he might have expected. He was consul-general in Chile from 1872 to 1878, and envoy extraordinary to Argentina, 1879 to 1881. Eventually in 1896 he was appointed ambassador in Vienna. Cf. item 303.

264. SHAW, Arthur E.

Forty years in the Argentine Republic. London, Elkin Mathews, Buenos Aires, Mitchell's Book Store, 1907. 229 p. Shaw first arrived in Argentina in 1864.

265. SPEARS, John Randolph

The gold-diggings of Cape Horn: a study of life in Tierra del Fuego and Patagonia. London and New York, G. P. Putnam's Sons, 1895. xi, 319 p. map, illus.

'It was as a reporter of the "Sun" of New York that I visited the region described . . .'—Author's preface.

266. TURNER, Thomas A.

Argentina and the Argentines; notes and impressions of a five years' sojourn in the Argentine Republic, 1885–90. London, Swan Sonnenschein, 1892. xvi, 370 p. illus.

267. WEBSTER, Stephen

Emigration to the River Plate, success of British subjects in Buenos Aires, list of landowners, description of the city and province of Buenos Aires, suitableness of the country to the capitalist, gentleman farmer, and labourer, with some account of the agricultural colonies of Santa Fe and Bahia Blanca. London, Bates and Hendy, 1871. 96 p.

'After a residence of many years in the River Plate . . .'— Page 3.

268. WHITE, Ernest William

Cameos from the silver land; or the experiences of a young naturalist in the Argentine Republic. 2 vols. London, John Van Voorst, 1881–82. xv, 412; xv, 527 p. map.

'. . . to place before my country men at home a true sketch of the Argentine Republic as it is.'—Author's preface.

(c) Brazil

269. ANDREWS, Christopher Columbus

Brazil, its conditions and prospects. New York, D. Appleton, 1887. 352 p.

A lawyer and politician, Andrews was U.S. consul-general in Rio de Janeiro 1882–85. In the 1891 edition, the following is added to the title: With an account of the downfall of the Empire, the establishment of the republic and the reciprocity treaty.

270. ASSU, Jacaré
Brazilian colonization from an European point of view.
London, Edward Stanford, 1873. 132 p.
A pseudonymous work. The British Museum files under
'Jacaré'.

271. BENNETT, Frank
Forty years in Brazil. London, Mills and Boon, 1914. xxiv,
271 p. illus.
Though the period mentioned clearly goes back well into the
nineteenth century, most of the information relates to the
twentieth century.

272. BROWN, Charles Barrington *and* LIDSTONE, William
Fifteen thousand miles on the Amazon and its tributaries.
London, Edward Stanford, 1878. xiii, 520 p. map, illus.
Brown and Lidstone went out to Brazil in 1873 to 'select and
report on certain territories allotted to the Amazon Steamship
Company'.

273. BURKE, Ulick Ralph *and* STAPLES, Robert (Junior)
Business and pleasure in Brazil. London, Field and Tuer, the
Leadenhalle Press, Hamilton, Adams, Simpkin and Marshall,
New York, Scribner and Welford, 1886. iv, 148 p.

274. CHURCH, George Earl
The route to Bolivia via the River Amazon. A report to the
governments of Bolivia and Brazil. London, printed by Water-
low, 1877. 216 p. maps.
'President of the National Bolivian Navigation Company and
Chairman of the Madeira and Mamoré Railway Company,
Limited'—Title-page.

275. CLOUGH, R. Stewart
The Amazons. Diary of a twelve-month's journey, on a mis-
sion of inquiry up the River Amazon for the South American
Missionary Society. London, South American Missionary
Society, 1872. 2, 238 p. illus.
The details are confirmed by the Library of Congress cata-
logue.

276. COOK, William Azel

Through the wildernesses of Brazil by horse, canoe and float. New York, American Tract Society, London, T. Fisher Unwin. iv, 487 p. illus.

The New York edition appeared in 1909, the London edition probably a year later. Werner of Akron, Ohio, published an edition in 1909 entitled: *By horse, canoe and float through the wildernesses of Brazil*.

Cook was a missionary. It is not clear when the actual journey took place.

277. DENT, Hastings Charles

A year in Brazil with notes on the abolition of slavery, the finances of the Empire, religion, meteorology, natural history, etc. London, Kegan Paul and Trench, 1886. xvii, 444 p. maps, illus.

278. FRANCES, May

Beyond the Argentine: or, letters from Brazil. London, W. H. Allen, 1890. viii, 148 p. map.

279. HUMPHREY, Alice R.

A summer journey to Brazil. New York, Bonnell and Silver, 1900. ix, 149 p. illus.

The author made several visits to Brazil during the reign of the Emperor Pedro II and the early republic.

280. MATHEWS, Edward Davis

Up the Amazon and Madeira rivers, through Bolivia and Peru. London, Sampson Low, Marston, Searle and Rivington, 1879. xv, 402 p. map, illus.

281. MULHALL, Michael George *and* MULHALL, Edward T.

Handbook of Brazil. Buenos Aires, 1877. 232, 4 p. illus.

No publisher is named. The authors are described on the title-page as 'editors of the *Standard*'. Included in the *Handbook* are two separate works by Michael George Mulhall.

(i) Journey to Matto Grosso. Buenos Aires, Printed and Published at the Standard Steam Printing Office, Standard Court. 67 p. illus.

(ii) Rio Grande do Sul and its German colonies. London, Longmans, Green, 1873. vi, 202 p. front.
Cf. item 138.

282. PETROS

A peep at Brazil. Buxton, J. C. Bates, Printer, 1876. 91 p.

283. SMITH, Herbert Huntington

Brazil, the Amazons and the coast. New York, Charles Scribner's Sons, 1879. xv, 644 p. map, illus.
Smith made two trips to the area in 1870 and 1874.

284. WELLS, James William

Exploring and travelling three thousand miles through Brazil from Rio de Janeiro to Maranhao. With an appendix containing statistics and observations on climate, railways, central sugar factories, mining, commerce and finance; the past, present and future, and physical geography of Brazil. 2 vols. Philadelphia, J. B. Lippincott, London, Sampson Low, Marston, Searle and Rivington, 1886.

285. WICKHAM, Henry Alexander

Rough notes of a journey through the wilderness, from Trinidad to Para, Brazil, by way of the great cataracts of the Orinoco, Atabapo and Rio Negro. London, W. J. H. Carter, 1872. xiv, 301 p. illus.
The first half of the book is about Brazil, the rest about Central America.

286. WITHER, Thomas Plantagenet Bigg-

Pioneering in South Brazil. Three years of forest and prairie life in the province of Parana. 2 vols. London, John Murray, 1878. xiii, 378; x, 328 p. map, illus.

287. WRIGHT, Marie Robinson

The new Brazil, its resources and attractions, historical, descriptive, and industrial. Philadelphia, George Barrie, London, C. D. Cazenove, 1901. 450 p. illus.
'... extended travels in Brazil, covering thousands of miles and requiring nearly two years for completion.'—Introduction.

288. WRIGHT, Walter

A few facts about Brazil by a twenty years' resident in that country. Birmingham, Cornish, London, Simpkin, Marshall, Hamilton and Kent, 1892. 53 p.
Published anonymously.

(d) West Coast

289. ACLAND, William (Commander R.N.)

Six weeks with the Chilean army, being a short account of a march from Pisco to Lurin, and the attack on Lima. 1880.
W. H. Koebel (*British exploits in South America*, New York, 1917) cites this item. He describes it as 'Privately printed at the Melanesian mission, Norfolk Island'. I have not been able to locate a copy.

290. AUBERTIN, John James

By order of the sun to Chile to see his total eclipse April 16, 1893. London, Kegan Paul, Trench and Trübner, 1894. 152 p. illus.
Also contains material on Peru and Bolivia.

291. BOYD, Robert Nelson

Chili; sketches of Chili and the Chilians during the war 1879–80. London, W. H. Allen, 1881. vii, 235 p. map, illus.
Contains some photographs.

292. CLARK, E. B.

Twelve months in Peru. London, T. Fisher Unwin, 1891. xxiii, 158 p. illus.

293. COLE, George R. FitzRoy

The Peruvians at home. London, Kegan Paul and Trench, 1884. xix, 277 p.
'In the spring of 1873, I had occasion to visit Peru on private business. I resided in that country for upwards of two years, during which time I had opportunities of seeing its most important towns and sights.'—Preface.

294. CONWAY, William Martin (Sir)

The Bolivian Andes. A record of climbing and exploration in the Cordillera Real in the years 1898 and 1900. New York, London, Harper, 1901. ix, 405 p. illus.

Conway travelled very widely, and in addition to being a mountaineer was a collector and art critic. *Cf.* item 218.

295. CURTIS, William Eleroy

Between the Andes and the Ocean. An account of an interesting journey down the West coast of South America from the Isthmus of Panama to the Straits of Magellan. Chicago, Herbert S. Stone, 1900. 442 p. illus.

The cover title is *From the Andes to the Ocean. Cf.* items 222 and 312.

296. DAHLGREN, Sarah Madeleine Vinton

South sea sketches. A narrative. Boston, James R. Osgood, 1881. 238 p.

Née Vinton, Mrs. Dahlgren was married to Rear-Admiral John Adolphus Dahlgren of the U.S. Navy. Her book contains material on Peru and Chile. She describes it as: 'an accurate account of the incidents of a residence in South America'.

297. DUFFIELD, Alexander James

Peru in the guano age: being a short account of a recent visit to the guano deposits with some reflections on the money they have produced and the uses to which it has been applied. London, Richard Bentley, 1877. 151 p.

Cf. items 226 and 298.

298. DUFFIELD, Alexander James

The prospects of Peru. The end of the guano age and a description thereof with some account of the guano deposits and 'nitrate' plains. London, Newman, 1881. 120 p.

Cf. items 226 and 297.

299. HERVEY, Maurice H.

Dark days in Chile. An account of the revolution of 1891. London, Edward Arnold, 1891–92. x, 331 p. illus.

Hervey was a *Times* correspondent. He describes his book as 'based upon notes made regularly and methodically in Chile'.

300. HUTCHINSON, Thomas Joseph

Two years in Peru, with exploration of its antiquities. 2 vols. London, Sampson Low, Marston, Low and Searle, 1873. xxiv, 343; xii, 334 p. map, illus.
Cf. items 130 and 131.

301. KENNEDY, William Robert (Captain later Admiral R.N.)

Sporting adventures in the Pacific, whilst in command of the 'Reindeer'. London, Sampson Low, Marston, Searle and Rivington, 1876. 303 p. illus.
Describes visits to some ports on the west coast of South America. *Cf.* item 234.

302. MARKHAM, Clements Robert (Sir)

Peru. London, Sampson Low, Marston, Searle and Rivington, 1880. viii, 192 p. map, illus.
Cf. items 188 and 189.

303. RUMBOLD, Horace (Sir)

Report on the progress and general condition of Chile. 1876.
This work was published as a 'blue book' presented to the two Houses of Parliament. *Cf.* item 263.

304. RUSSELL, William Howard (Sir)

A visit to Chile and the nitrate fields of Tarapaca etc. London, J. S. Virtue, 1890. xii, 374 p. map, illus.
From 1841 to 1863, Russell was a war correspondent of *The Times*.

305. SEEBEE, Felix

Travelling impressions in, and notes on, Peru. London, Elliot Stock, 1901. 196 p. map.
Seebee does not state exactly when his travels took place. But his 'last experiences in Peru were from 1880 to 1881'. He gives some account of incidents in the Guerra del Pacifico, in particular the capture of Lima by the Chilean forces.

306. SIMSON, Alfred

Travels in the wilds of Ecuador and the exploration of the Putumayo river. London, Sampson Low, Marston, Searle and Rivington, 1886. v, 270 p. map.

307. SMITH, William Anderson

Temperate Chile: a progressive Spain. London, Adam and Charles Black, 1899. x, 399 p. map, front.
Based on first-hand experience of the country.

308. SQUIER, Ephraim George

Peru. Incidents of travel and exploration in the land of the Incas. London, Macmillan, 1877. xx, 599 p. map, illus.
Squier was a journalist, diplomat and archaeologist, and was largely self-educated. His early work as an archaeologist was on native remains in the United States. In 1849, he was appointed chargé d'affaires in Central America, partly through the influence of W. H. Prescott. His work in and on Central America was distinguished by its anti-British character. From 1863 to 1865, he was U.S. commissioner to Peru.

309. WHYMPER, Edward

Travels amongst the great Andes of the Equator. London, John Murray, 1892. xxiv, 456 p. maps, illus.
Whymper was a wood engraver and an alpinist. He climbed Chimborazo and Cotopaxi as well as visiting Quito. The book contains a supplementary appendix (xxii, 147 p.). A title-page to this appendix carries the date of publication 1891.

310. WILMOT Sydney Marow Eardley-

Our journal in the Pacific. By the officers of H.M.S. 'Zealous'. Arranged and edited by Lieutenant S. Eardley-Wilmot. London, Longmans, Green, 1873. xiv, 353, xx p. map, illus.

(e) North

311. BARRY, William

Venezuela: a visit to the gold mines of Guyana, and voyages up the river Orinoco during 1886, with a brief sketch of the mineral wealth and resources of Venezuela and its history to the present time. With a map of the mines; and appendices containing the mining laws of Venezuela, report on the mines by the Minister of War, Extract from British Consular Reports, and an outline of the clauses of treaties under which Great Britain claims certain territorics on the Essequibo. London, Marshall, 1886. 159, lxxviii p. map.

312. CURTIS, William Eleroy

Venezuela; a land where it's always summer. New York, Harper, 1896. 315 p. map.

Also a London edition, Osgood, McIlvaine, 1896. 315 p. *Cf*. items 222 and 295.

313. DANCE, Charles Daniel

Recollections of four years in Venezuela. London, Henry S. King, 1876. xii, 303 p. map, illus.

314. DAVIS, Richard Harding

Three gringos in Venezuela and Central America. New York, Harper, 1896. xi, 282 p. map, illus.

Davis is described by the *Dictionary of American Biography* as 'the most widely known reporter of his generation'. The last chapter is about Venezuela.

315. MILLICAN, Albert

Travels and adventures of an orchid hunter. An account of canoe and camp life in Colombia, while collecting orchids in the Northern Andes. London, Paris, Melbourne, Cassell, 1891. xv, 222 p. illus.

316. MORRIS, Ira Nelson

With the trade winds. A jaunt in Venezuela and the West Indies. New York, London, G. P. Putnam's Sons, 1897. x, 157 p. illus.

An account of Venezuela occupies pages 90 to 157.

317. SPENCE, James Mudie

The land of Bolivar or war, peace, and adventure in the

republic of Venezuela. 2 vols. London, Sampson Low, Marston, Searle and Rivington, 1878. xx, 323; x, 343 p. maps, illus.

318. WEARS, W. G.

The prospects of gold mining in Venezuela. London, printed for private circulation by W. W. Head and Mark, 1888. 58 p. map.

'. . . based on an experience of six years connection with the mining industry in that country . . .'—Preface.

319. WILLIAMS, Rosa Carnegie

A year in the Andes or A lady's adventures in Bogota. London, London Literary Society, (1882?). 270 p.

The British Museum describes this as 'Printed 1884'.

320. WOOD, Walter E.

Venezuela; or two years on the Spanish Main. London, Simpkin, Marshall, Hamilton, Kent, Middlesbrough, Jordison, 1896. [4], xxxii, 196 p. map, illus.

APPENDIX

Outstanding Nineteenth-Century Translations

AI. ADALBERT (Prince, of Prussia)

Travels of His Royal Highness Prince Adalbert of Prussia in the south of Europe and in Brazil, with a voyage up the Amazon and Xingu. Translated by Sir Robert H. Schomburgk and John Edward Taylor. 2 vols. London, D. Bogue, 1849. maps.

A2. DAUXION-LAVAYSSE, Jean François

A statistical, commercial, and political description of Venezuela, Trinidad, Margarita, and Tobago: containing various anecdotes and observations, illustrative of the past and present state of these interesting countries: from the French of M. Lavaysse: with an introduction and explanatory notes by the editor. London, G. and W. B. Whittaker, 1820. xxxix, 479 p. maps.

A3. GERSTÄCKER, Friedrich Wilhelm Christian

Narrative of a journey round the world, comprising a winter-passage across the Andes to Chili, with a visit to the gold regions of California and Australia, the South Sea islands, Java, etc. 3 vols. London, Hurst and Blackett, 1853.

Also a one-volume edition in the same year by Harper of New York (624 p.)

A4. HELMS, Anton Zacharias

Travels from Buenos Ayres, by Potosi, to Lima. With notes by the translator, containing topographical descriptions of the Spanish possessions in South America, drawn from the last and best authorities. London, R. Phillips, 1806. xii, 287 p.

Also contains extracts from Alcedo and Ulloa. There was an 1807 edition by Phillips (92 p.).

A5. HUMBOLDT, Alexander von

Personal narrative of travels to the equinoctial regions of the New continent, during the years 1799–1804. By Alexander de Humboldt, and Aimé Bonpland ... written in French by Alexander de Humboldt, and translated into English by Helen Maria Williams. 7 volumes in 9. London, Longman, Hurst, Rees, Orme, and Brown. 1814–29. maps, illus.

This widely read work went through several editions in nineteenth-century Britain and the United States.

A6. KELLER-LEUZINGER, Franz

The Amazon and Madeira rivers; sketches and descriptions from the notebook of an explorer. New York, D. Appleton, London, Chapman and Hall, 1874. xvi, 177 p. illus.

A7. LANGSDORFF, George Heinrich von

Voyages and travels in various parts of the world, during the years 1803, 1804, 1805, 1806, and 1807. 2 vols. London, H. Colburn, 1813–14. map. illus.

Also a one-volume U.S. edition (xvi, 617 p.) in 1817.

A8. MAXIMILIAN I, of Mexico

Recollections of my life. 3 vols. London, R. Bentley, 1868. Volume 3 contains an account of Brazil.

A9. MOLLIEN, Gaspard Theodore

Travels in the republic of Colombia, in the years 1822 and 1823. London, C. Knight, 1824. iv, 460 p. map, front. Translated from the French.

A10. NUÑEZ, Ignacio Benito

An account, historical, political, and statistical, of the United Provinces of Rio de la Plata: with an appendix, concerning the usurpation of Monte Video by the Portuguese and Brazilian governments. London, Printed for R. Ackermann, 1825. x, 345 p.

'Translated from the Spanish'—Note on the title-page.

A11. PAEZ, Ramon

Wild scenes in South America; or, Life in the llanos of Venezuela. New York, C. Scribner, 1862. x, 502 p. illus.

Paez was a native of South America. But he was a friend of Waterton and acknowledged the debt he owed for his education to 'the learned fathers at the College of Stonyhurst'. The book saw later editions, some entitled: *Travels and adventures in South and Central America.*

A12. PAZOS KANKI, Vicente

Letters on the United provinces of South America, addressed to the Hon. Henry Clay, speaker of the House of Representatives in the United States. Translated from the Spanish by Platt H. Crosby, esq. New York, J. Seymour, London, J. Miller, 1819. xi, 259 p. map.

A13. PFEIFFER, Ida

A lady's voyage round the world: a selected translation from the German of Ida Pfeiffer. By Mrs. Percy Sinnett. New York, Harper, 1852. 302 p.

A14. PFEIFFER, Ida

A lady's second journey round the world: from London to the Cape of Good Hope, Borneo, Java, Sumatra, Celebes, Ceram, the Moluccas, etc., California, Panama, Peru, Ecuador and the United States. New York, Harper, 1856. xii, 500 p.

A15. PONS, François Raymond Joseph de

Travels in South America during the years 1801, 1802, 1803, and 1804; containing a description of the captain-generalship of Caraccas and an account of the discovery, conquest, topography, legislature, commerce, finance and natural productions of the country; with a view of the manners and customs of the Spaniards and the native Indians. Translated from the French. 2 vols. London, Longman, Hurst, Rees, and Orme, 1807. map.

R. Phillips had published an abridged translation in 1806 in the first series of *A collection of modern and contemporary voyages and travels*.

A16. RENGGER, Johann Rudolph

The reign of Doctor Joseph Gaspard Roderick de Francia, in Paraguay; being an account of six years' residence in that republic, from July, 1819—to May, 1825. By Messrs. Rengger and Longchamps. Translated from the French of J. R. Rengger. London, T. Hurst, E. Chance, 1827. xvi, 208 p.

A17. SAINT CRICQ, Laurent

Travels in South America from the Pacific ocean to the Atlantic ocean. By Paul Marcoy. 2 vols. London, Blackie, 1875. maps, illus.
Translated from the French by Elihu Rich.

A18. SARMIENTO, Domingo Faustino

Life in the Argentine republic in the days of the tyrants; or, Civilization and barbarism. From the Spanish of Domingo F. Sarmiento. With a biographical sketch of the author, by Mrs. Horace Mann. New York, Hurd and Houghton, 1868. xxxv, 400 p. front.

A19. SPIX, Johann Baptist von *and* MARTIUS, Karl Friedrich Philipp von

Travels in Brazil, in the years 1817–20. Undertaken by command of His Majesty the King of Bavaria. By Dr. Johann Baptist von Spix and Dr. C. F. P. von Martius. Translated by H. E. Lloyd. 2 volumes in 1. London, Longman, Hurst, Rees, Orme, Brown, and Green, 1824.

A20. TSCHUDI, Johann Jakob von

Travels in Peru, during the years 1838–42. Translated from the German by Thomasina Ross. London, D. Bogue, 1847. xii, 606 p. front.
Also a New York edition (Wiley and Putnam) in the same year.

A21. WIED-NEUWIED, Maximilian Alexander Philipp, Prinz von

Travels in Brazil in the years 1815, 1816, 1817. Part I. London, R. Phillips, 1820.

Part I (iv, 112 p.) was the only one published. Colburn also published this in the same year.

AUTHOR INDEX

(Numbers prefixed by the letter A are in the appendix of translations)